WIDE SKY, NARROW PATH

WIDE SKY, NARROW PATH

A View From The Trail

Courtney Lynne Mann

To order additional copies of this book, contact:
Xlibris Corporation
1-888-795-4274
www.Xlibris.com
Orders@Xlibris.com
86890

Contents

For Uncle Ed.

"Tot mai citesti probleme sociale . . .
Sau, ce mai scrii, iubita mea uitata?"

Acknowledgments

While Brad Mann first introduced me to the Appalachian Trail and David Mann equipped me for it, I could not have started the long path without Will "Gollum" Spotts, finished it without Robert "Yukon" Stubblebine, or sustained it without the prayers of many.

Likewise, the architecture of this book would not be complete without the input of some wonderfully talented authors and editors: with great thanks to Jen Waddell, for generous inspiration through the years and dynamic, faithful and provocative writers' group leadership; David Manuel, for helping articulate the organizational backbone of the narrative; Al Lilliendahl for writerly wisdom and wordsmithing refinement; Liz DeBarros, for poignant literary perception and the ongoing dialogue of hope; Tom Brodeur, for graciously plowing through an early rough-hewn manuscript; Odessa Criales-Smith, for spiritual discernment and foundational critique; Jim Schaad, for owl sessions refining past and present participles ("*do* talk to me about grammar!") fluency in the language of creative process and many years of artistic encouragement; and most of all, thanks to my wonderful parents, Dr. Richard and Vonda Mann: dad, for tireless logistical support, countless Beavins Road reminders and ceaselessly cheering me on; mom, for an educator's refining wisdom, poetic wit and tenacious editorial moxie.

Special thanks are due Enid Woods for prayer support during the hike—I might not be here to share this were it not for your prayers; Bill Aliberti, Doris McLaughlin and Pam Oehlberg, for spirit-led mentorship; David Lenk, for reminding me that the goal validates the struggle; Danyelle Pearson, for nurturing possibilities; Steve Rapson, for insight into editing and process; Taylor Stokes, for writerly wisdom and grace; Jeff Sellenrick, for enduring text-to-speech readings, and celebrating milestones along the way; "Wake" Jared Baskey, for the O-ring reminder and rocket launch countdown; Elizabeth Siesel, for timely musings and hopester inspiration;

Hetty White, for much-needed laughter and intercession; Rick Fleeter, for a lion's share of authorly wisdom, humor, and wit; and Eric and Tara Mann, for dark chocolate and solidarity along the way.

In affectionate memory of Max Lynn Woods, for daring me to finish the trail, and writing provocateurs Howard Henke and Helen Maude Sterling, for ceaselessly believing in and inspiring me to publish these stories.

In remembrance of Emily Elizabeth Roe, whose footprints leave an indelible trail of the power of grace.

Most of all, I thank my Creator for the gift of walking, the gift of writing, and the joyous gift of life.

Dedicated to hiking partners Gollum, Pilgrim, Oasis, Purple, Nocona, Hawaii, Half Calf, Gugumug, Crackerjack, Washboard, Monkhead, Tin Man, Wardog, Katydid, Real Bill, Glacier, the rest of the inimitable Class of 1998, and to all who call the trail home.

Oh, these vast, calm, measureless mountain days, inciting at once to work and rest! Days in whose light everything seems equally divine, opening a thousand windows to show us God. Nevermore, however weary, should one faint by the way who gains the blessings of one mountain day; whatever his fate, long life, short life, stormy or calm, he is rich forever.

~John Muir

Introduction

To be alive at all is to traverse some kind of a trail, with passages through shadows and sun, devastation and hope, and the clarity that only comes through hindsight.

When I set out to journey more than 2,000 miles on foot across the Appalachian ridgeline from Georgia bound for Maine, little did I know a simple path cutting its way through the woods would carry me to places within I had never been before, and perhaps could not have reached any other way. However, to say that the long walk was rewarded with delights and hardships unique to the terrain and company kept does not necessarily give great insight into the peculiarities of long-distance hiking; the same could be said of any chosen and sustained way.

Over the course of seven months, the thru-hike became a living collection of epiphanies tethered to the practicalities of sweat and soil; a grand metaphor for life, and an enduring point of reference. However, recalling and writing of the trail was far less linear than walking it. As your eyes rove over these thoughtscapes, may you capture some essence of the adventure and glimpse enduring parallels to your own journey, whatever the timeline or circumstance.

To dare is to momentarily lose one's footing; not to dare is to lose oneself.

Søren Kierkegaard

one | The Threshold

If a journey of a thousand miles begins with one step, perhaps a journey of two thousand, one hundred and sixty-seven miles begins with two. For every step on soil along the trail, a second indelible footprint was pressed into the *substance of things hoped for, the evidence of things not seen.* A walk of faith.

The first time I heard about the hardy few who walked the Appalachian Trail's length in one continuous journey, I considered them an elite assemblage, and hardly worthy of their ranks. Nevertheless, I was intrigued by such daring, and inspired perhaps most of all by the somewhat absurd nature of the quest.

Several years came and went before a convergence of curiosity, desire and circumstance led not only to exploring the prospect of a thru-hike but to the place where it didn't seem an option *not* to try. Having spent no more than five overnights backpacking at any one time hardly seemed an indicator of the stamina such an effort would require. But at the very least, it was a bold step toward the center of desire.

The road leading to the trailhead had been a thorny one: creative aspirations displaced by discouragement; romance gone awry; a growing sense of existential inertia. Driving the desire to move from the shadowy comfort of things familiar was the fear of never fulfilling deepest yearnings. The decision to fill a pack with only essentials and go tread the backs of the mountains for an extended time was a declaration to all other fronts of life that the way things had been was not the way things had to stay.

Stepping over the threshold of this new beginning seemed like some sort of a test: would I pass or would I fail? And what exactly was the criterion for success? I found it could not be measured in miles or effort, but rather, in desire: to awaken, to live fully, freely and according to truest design. To leave all that was familiar in search of a life more deliberately lived was the beginning of that freedom.

Reflecting on the random circumstances which led to the decision to go, it was as if an unseen hand had quietly been aligning all the tumblers in a lock on the door that led to the life I had always sensed was mine but had somehow never been able to open. Close to throwing the ineffective key away, one day, trying it again out of sheer frustration, the tumblers mysteriously clicked into place and the door fell open.

The same door that opened to the new closed on the old.

While tempted to toss it, I kept the key. I later found it was a sort of skeleton key with the ability to open many other doors.

License Plates

Three more weeks at home in Boston and I would be on my way: a plane to Atlanta, a bus to Gainesville, a shuttle van to Amicalola Falls, and my own feet to Maine. My backpack leaned against the wall, stretched to the seams with tent, sleeping bag, stove, and a colorful assortment of nylon stuff-sacks full of best guesses as to bare necessities. If the weight of my backpack was going to be too great to walk easily, or too little to camp comfortably, time would soon tell. Everything else in my apartment had been boxed up; life as I had known it was going to be put on indefinite hold.

Yet despite all the dreaming, longing and planning, it still seemed I was stepping off a well-lit path into wasteland. Pulling the door closed on the way out for some last-minute errands, I felt a growing anxiousness as I considered what was soon to begin. I had quit my job and packed up my home to walk in the woods for an inordinate length of time. With the mounting sense of frustration I found myself uttering: "God! What is my purpose in life? What do you want me to do? If you would just tell me, I'd do it! If you're real, then make it clear—bring it on!" I did not expect an immediate response.

Stepping out of the dimly lit foyer of my apartment building into the bright sunlight, I headed for the train. As I passed the Salvation Army thrift store a block down the street, two cars parked bumper to bumper in front of the shop suddenly caught my gaze. The first car had Georgia license plates; and the second car: Maine plates. The effect was no less profound than if I'd audibly heard, "Here's what I have for you to do. Do it! The rest will be just as plainly revealed in time."

While it seemed a bit daft and wildly narcissistic to assume such happenstance could have been orchestrated just for me, a stray hope welled within. Just as with the unknowns surrounding the forthcoming hike itself, I decided I had nothing to lose in suspending my doubt.

If I could believe in One immense enough to create all which is, must not that Being also be as powerfully small? Somewhere between the two infinite and undiminished extremes, perhaps we can so meet, and be met.

Cold March

The advent of the hike was cold, blustery and somewhat foreboding; local news reported tornados and the loss of several lives and many homes in the vicinity of the trail's southern terminus.

Donning full hiker regalia in all its synthetic-fiber splendor that first morning felt more like preparation for some unnamed battle than taking first steps into pure freedom. Swells of ice along the rocky corridor the first few miles were an unavoidable reminder that it might be the first month of spring in Georgia, but it was still winter in the mountains. Would my thin rain shell, the only consistent shelter I would have during each day's walk hold up through an eight-hour downpour? Would my tent leak? Would my 20 degree sleeping bag keep me warm at night?

The otherwise uneventful day ended at the shelter area overflowing with a large crowd of aspiring thru-hikers and all the awkwardness of the first day of school. Perfect strangers representing every level of outdoor experience, ineptitude and gumption pretending not to notice we were all in too close proximity for comfort, decked out in the latest gear, industriously setting up camp: pumping water, stringing clothes lines, pitching tents, firing up camp stoves like trail-hardened veterans, a scant four and a half miles into two thousand.

I watched a young couple go to elaborate lengths to sterilize a shiny new cooking pot, supposing my simpler "kitchen" habits to be inferior. I had been particularly impressed and intimidated watching them boil extra water and generously load tiny sponges with camp soap, not knowing that too much can cause very unpleasant gastrological side effects. Not to mention the next time the pot is used, boiling water does its job. There was no way of knowing at the time my particular method was the one most commonly practiced by the majority of long-distance hikers.

Sometimes we doubt our own method, but simple efficiencies are usually the most brilliant, regardless of whether or not they are so acknowledged. Fine-tuning of gear along the trail increases with time, and processes that seem to befuddle when new soon become streamlined and subconscious.

By far the most unusual dishwashing technique I witnessed on the trail was that of a veteran on his third or fourth thru-hike. He had his kitchen ritual down to a somewhat unappetizing if not intriguing routine. After scraping up the last bits of dinner from the sides of his pot, he would pour in just enough water to the remains to make a cup of hot cocoa. Stirred the chocolate powder in, drank it all down. Then the bit of genius hard to watch: he scoured the pot clean with his toothbrush. Sucked the specks out of the toothbrush. Added just enough water to rinse out the pot, clean the toothbrush, drink the water, brush his teeth. Not a speck of food, drop of water, or calorie wasted.

Profile of a Trail

Remote for detachment, narrow for chosen company, winding for leisure, lonely for contemplation, the Trail beckons not merely north and south but upward to the body, mind and soul of man. Often seen in print in trail-related literature, and commonly credited to his fellow visionaries, Harold Allen's eloquent words frame the trail's purpose not so much in terms of physical rigors as in spiritual sojourn, and rightly so. The Appalachian Trail naturally has certain distinctions that set it apart from all other trails. But like any path, it is simply a focused place to walk to reach an intended destination.

The vision which brought the Appalachian Trail into being was by design a means of creating a gateway to experience life outside humanly constructed confines, to learn what can only be experienced out-of-doors, fully immersed in creation. The trail experience draws equally upon the heart, spirit and mind, allowing for a unique harmonization to take place. Perhaps one of its greatest lessons was to see the value of being led into something new, and rather than being undone by it, to enjoy stepping into the unknown.

The events of the trail are perfect mirrors to lift outside of time and place, in order to glimpse truths that can shed light on any path, anywhere. The trail itself is neither easy nor hard; it is simply there. And although it may be host to many challenges, the choice to walk upon its narrow way is rewarded with delights known only to those who find themselves so immersed.

Leaving the familiarities of urban life to walk through the trees puts the long-distance hiker back in touch with a much more primal experience of living and brings about a shift in worldview that perhaps transcends the physical experience of the hike. The trail ushers in a new season of forgoing the status quo for a clearer vision. It is an abundant time to cultivate dreams and hopes perhaps extinguished by the monotonous duties of everyday life; an ascent into essence.

Never knowing what is around the next literal bend in the trail despite maps, profile elevations and guidebook details is much of its lure. This fact alone could make the experience intimidating, but there is a kind of resident friendliness about the trail. To gaze at it is to be beckoned, and we move out upon it as if hoping to walk straight into our destiny, as if a physical path could so order our life. While the thru-hiking experience is different things for different people, among other elements, it is a kind of life-primer of the stuff no mere human construct could ever teach. It is a place to cultivate understanding on a level deeper than intellect alone; a place to learn the ways of the spirit and of the heart.

An intensely concentrated interval of time in which the usual distractions of life are left behind for a very simple day-to-day existence, the thru-hike allows enough space in between events to let such awareness naturally come, like seedlings reaching towards the light once weeds have been cleared. Lessons learned and wisdom gained are ushered in to the degree that there is openness to follow wherever the path leads. And even as the way becomes more familiar, there is still newness to discover all along the way.

The distractions and encumbrances of life lived unconsciously can eventually bury the life of the spirit. The trail is like a blank page for all the unexpressed thoughts and emotions otherwise held back in an environment where busyness keeps our minds too crowded to even know what we feel or deeply dream.

It is ironic that going out of the indoors and getting filthy beyond belief allows for a cleansing to occur. And while it may be far from most people's minds when setting out to hike, the long walk by its nature imposes certain disciplines that practiced over time encourages a greater resiliency to life lived either on or off the trail. The thru-hike is like a boot camp for reawakening, though it may be a difficult sell to someone who doesn't like being insect bait or not bathing for days on end. Hikers don't necessarily enjoy showerlessness or bugs any more than anyone else, but may have a greater tolerance for them! This in fact may be the key prerequisite to thru-hike.

The elements that otherwise make the thru-hike possible are straightforward enough: the necessary equipment and resolve to walk it. Gear is designed to be stronger, lighter and smarter with each passing year, but like the trail itself, is only a means to an end. The beginning is wilderness, itself a means and an open door to the ongoing end of a civilized soul.

A backpacker straps on a physical weight in exchange for the weightlessness of other burdens released.

Some have never darkened the doorstep of an outfitter store or walked down a physical trail, let alone slept in the woods for months on end. Others feel unable to hike for lack of physical fitness. However, the only needful ingredients to hike outside of time are willingness to do it, a certain relish for risk, and a desire to tip the scale into full abandonment. Sometimes we wonder if we have the stamina to accomplish a task laid before us. But strengthening generally comes *as* we go, not before. Being fit is not what makes the hike possible; it is merely a factor of how comfortable it will be at the start. The body adapts supremely well to what might otherwise seem like punishment taken out of context. And it is helpful to remind oneself that it is nearly impossible to conceive before it happens of just how good it feels once the rhythm of the walk has been established.

And as we continue on our way, the direction we are to travel becomes clear, one single step at a time.

With all its unknowns and changing vistas, the trail is a reminder that any day lived anywhere is an invitation to look deeper into all we experience and see the possibilities that only seem to not exist when we rush past. Regardless of circumstance and surroundings, we are all travelers: only gear, terrain and duration of the journey vary. And no matter what the ultimate outcome, adventure is a risk worth taking, with new insights to be gained.

The trail doesn't have to end after the last blaze;[1] it continues on to the extent that it cultivates hunger for more forays into the unknown and a greater appreciation for the beauty all around to be seen. And whether this beauty takes the form of difficult lessons learned, new joys discovered or more mysteries to solve—captivating truths are just waiting to be uncovered.

Adventure takes us to the brink of ourselves, to the very edge of self and societally imposed limits, flaunting a new and unknown path. Those who

---

[1]   From end to end, the entire Appalachian Trail is 'blazed' or marked with white rectangular stripes of two by six inches, painted at regular intervals on trees and rocks to identify the path.

thirst for change, vitality, and experiencing life as fully as possible find the call into the unknown irresistible. Our core drive for survival is rarely called upon in our overly insulated lifestyles, and like an unused muscle, atrophies. The trail tones that muscle, and we find a greater zeal to be alive, to be free, with a more authentic appreciation for small things perhaps overlooked in the past.

The trail offers countless seeds of insight for the taking, only requiring that we walk to them and take what can be received. There is no prescripted way to hike, and no two journeys are the same. We all have something to teach and something to learn. But perhaps the lessons best learned come in wordless forms.

Through wilderness passages and ridgelines, respite in towns and villages, through rain, snow and sun and the elation of reaching another summit, the long hike is a journey like any, full of hopes, mishaps, wild expectations, surprises, accidents and triumphs. Despite its many challenges, remaining with the experience to the end, wherever that happens to be, inspires a greater courage and faith for whatever lies ahead.

Metaphors Be With You

Signs are silent heralds intended to give direction, or at times stand as memorials, directing steps of a different kind by commemorating a path previously taken. Signs and sojourners go hand in hand.

Countless signs announce the trail and its related sideshows: the next scenic overlook. The side trail to the water source. The path to the privy. Distance to the next shelter or the next road crossing. Old homesteads and grave sites. The halfway point, and ultimately the distance from one end of the trail to the other.

There is a certain comfort in knowing that despite its constant unpredictability, the trail is measured. To walk it at all is to go with the knowing that the path is finite and one day the walking will be done. The simple math of knowing that each sign passed is one sign closer to the goal, anchoring every aspect of the journey. The trail itself is both the reason for experiencing what happens along the way, and the portal to it. It is profoundly rich and complete because it is both means and end.

Yet the trail does not always lead through pleasant passages and for all its natural splendors is at times a place of drudgery, questioning, and even disaster. Signs are assurances that one is still on the path, and that if others have successfully passed through, others can as well.

For northbound thru-hikers, the most favored sign and memorial of all is at trail's end on Mount Katahdin. Wind-battered, storm-weathered, the sign's face is scarred with initials of many pilgrims, etched like laugh lines in an old face. It is an altar to the joy of a long-sought goal finally accomplished, all the sweeter for the challenges encountered to reach it.

About two hundred miles into the hike, I walked past a truck parked at a trailhead with a bumper sticker that read: "Metaphors Be With You." The trail indeed presented ceaselessly fruitful opportunities to observe how even the most trivial of events can yield life principles, some with the power to change the course of one's life.

The long way is filled with innumerable examples of the mysteries that wrap around our limited understanding. The physicality of the trail is balanced by an almost perpetual transcendence of spirit. Harmony with the natural realm is cultivated with each mile deeper into undomesticated terrain, the path itself the one ordered line through the tangled mystery of the woods and all it harbors. It is an unparalleled sanctuary to both contemplate creation and commune with what no human hands have made.

The trail echoes the spiritual and psychological heights, delights and rock bottom lows of the pathway of consciousness as the thru-hiker stumbles, soars and sweats through an unforgettable two thousand mile walk. Along with rich memories and friendships forged, there is an abundance of time to once again believe that dreams are an integral part of existence, and sometimes need patience and space to be resurrected. To become plans.

Thousands hike the trail one way or another; by section, by day or end-to-end. Its difficulty lies more in the preparation and pruning away of time and resources and relationships to make way for it to happen, than the actual hike itself. Yet as an intentionally chosen path, the effort required to follow through ultimately replenishes the soul. Despite struggles along the way, joy remains the overriding temper of the trail: it is a gift just to be there making the attempt to walk any portion of its length.

There were places along the trail in northern New England where the climbs and even more so the rocky descents were so steep, the path seemed virtually impassable. I would stand at such junctures looking down a sheer vertical drop and wonder how it could possibly be navigated while remaining in one piece. Feeling somewhat marooned and wishing I could give the builder of that particular section of trail a piece of my mind, I would first peer down the embankment and then immediately remind myself that there were no hiker bodies or skeletons jumbled at the base of the drop. Nor was there any queue either in front of or behind me of other hikers asking the same question. Armed with this thought, despite the fact that gravity did not seem to be on my side, I would somehow manage to climb down using fissures in the rock and bordering roots or saplings as makeshift ladder rungs. There was always a way, even when there seemed no way.

Not Exactly a Thoreau-Hike

Most hikers seek time in the woods to find out what it means to live with intentionality, or at the least, to figure out how to. More than just strapping on a pack and thinning one's boot soles over absurd distances, the thru-hike is about shedding expectations of what it means to live a meaningful existence, by a deliberate return to simplicity, even primitivism, for a period of time. It is a time of recalibration.

Most hikers would probably affirm Thoreau's rationale for stepping away from ordinary life, even if for just a season: *I went to the woods because I wished to live deliberately, to front only the essential facts of life, and see if I could not learn what it had to teach, and not, when I came to die, discover that I had not lived.* Despite a certain shared austerity, one major distinction that sets the long walk apart from Thoreau's quest is the element of constant movement. It is a reminder of not yet having come to a resting place. Yet resting along the way is as important as the walk, not only to regain strength and to strategize, but to reflect; to fully notice and therefore enjoy the progress made. Resting requires the discipline and conscious decision to not push harder than the day requires.

Depending on the terrain, it is possible to settle into a meditative and deeply restful pace as the visual rhythm of leaf and shadow, stone and soil blend with the walking and hours go by unnoticed, one's thoughts roving along above the trail like a kite in the wind.

In those moments, there can be an overwhelming sense of being a part of the rhythm of the woods so as to completely lose a sense of otherness from the rest of creation. What felt like self-oblivion was perhaps not so much an unawareness or forgetting as much as a connecting to the greater whole. At such times, everything is best understood in a larger context where differences are transcended, and all things are seen as they truly are, held together by an ineffable hand.

The trail is a silent mentor for lessons uniquely received in the humility found out-of-doors: an artless classroom of the simple stuff of being. It begins with a love and longing for the journey and all the wonders of the natural world for undiminished stretches of time; complete immersion in the gallery of God outside the walls of human constructs.

Like the subtlest of teachers, the trail is unimposing, with a certain transparency, allowing only the essence of a thing to come to light. At times there were inexplicable bursts of insight, as if it were possible to see a million tiny particles of meaning dancing on each and every leaf, quiet as moonlight, not attempting to draw or convince, yet nevertheless profoundly felt. Some of life's greatest moments are made from such awareness that alights before disappearing just as suddenly against the elusive backdrop of time and space.

Countless thoughts take shape under the daily tattoo of boot tread, pressing textured patterns into the soil, temporary imprints to soon be modified by dainty mouse prints or definitive deer hooves. How many times has the earth been impressed with the random footprint, either human or animal, a momentary signature of existence, so utterly alike and unlike any other on the planet?

These are the kinds of ponderings the mind carries through the air by earthbound feet on a mammoth walk. Our collective stories are written in the soil as we go, interspersed with all the cravings a body could possible muster for the food beyond hiker range, many paces removed from the extravagant offering of town. We find ourselves confronting a constant polarity: on one hand, reveling in the green, growing world all around, far removed from the restless eye of society. And yet, as creatures of habit, this is balanced by the moments that we would willingly sell our birthright to this wild freedom for pizza and a cold beer. The trail is like a long, thin stretch of notebook paper that captures the ink of such thoughts.

But fortunately for the dedicated thru-hiker, even if the body demands to be released from the austere path in favor of more indulgent comforts, instant gratification is not usually an option. While there are some exceptions, deep in the woods is usually far away not only from the coveted store, local diner or hotel, but also from a road that may be still many more miles away from the closest outpost. The swish of nylon and click of a walking stick meeting stone becomes a kind of daily mantra as we simply walk on to the end of the day where we can finally lay our burden down and rest.

All I have seen teaches me to trust the Creator for all I have not seen.

Ralph Waldo Emerson

| *two* | Life in Three Dimensions |

A living map held just at arm's length, the trail is earthy and tangible as the sting of sweat seeping into the eyes after a long uphill push; the first sharp breath of early morning air after a stuffy night in the tent. It is burning the tip of the tongue on the first taste of hot noodles eating with one glove removed under cold, clear starlight; it is the scent of soil and leafy duff baking in the sunlight; the mingling fragrance of new sweat and damp of the woodland garden. We breathe in the atmosphere with the wind of the Creator in our lungs, releasing our own body climate into the air and earthen body all around us; it is a deep remembrance that we were never separate to begin with. Sweating is the baptism of effort, a release from head to toe. A cleansing takes place as the physical body is emboldened to movement by the urging of the soul. It is expressed in the soaring views from the top of a mountain with a view across the treetops of the distance traveled, all the sweeter for the effort to get there; it is released in the soul-satisfying rest after a crushingly long day hauling reluctant weight up and over uncountable hills.

One can go places both physically and spiritually with boots and a backpack that could never be reached through other means. The weight, the bulk and the burden are the transport by which one travels to places no car, bus, plane or train could ever go. Hidden in the rigors of trail life is a kind of zeal for purity and simplicity which may be buried under many years and layers of anxieties and distractions to varying degrees in different people.

Hiking the trail is like shedding a cocoon: the long walk offers countless opportunities to coax the soul out of hiding. The trail has just enough space to rethink the trajectory of one's life and allow for a sea change to take place; a chance to walk another direction, into a whole new beginning.

But it requires fuel.

All You Can Eat

If there is one obsession the thru-hiking community shares as much as the walk, it would be food. The average long-distance hiker likely thinks more about eating than anything else. Inordinate amounts of food are consumed at local diners and all-you-can-eat buffets in trailside towns, along with other delicacies that won't survive riding in a backpack for a week at a time. Even visiting the post office is somewhat of a culinary affair. While many hikers have food and supplies sent to post offices along the entire trail and walk according to a weekly mail drop schedule, some prefer to take the chance of resupplying at stores along the way rather than be limited to walking according to the hours of the post office. A resupply is all about getting as much food necessary as possible to take oneself only to the next town. You can't carry all that you need for the whole journey, but just enough to make it to the next stop. Standing in the grocery store can be mesmerizing: so much food, such a tremendous appetite yet so little space in a backpack.

We are given bountiful choices and opportunities all along the pathway of our lives, all and more than we could possibly consume. We do not always notice them: we are not always looking for them, or sometimes we are not looking in the right direction. But they are there, and are often only identified at resting points that are the necessary interruptions to our busyness. If we don't take the time to pause and reconfigure, we become weary, burnt out, more susceptible to injury—and at the very least, hungry to experience true meaning.

In contrast, when we consume more than we need, ordinary life becomes tasteless, mundane. It then takes more consumption to offset the boredom, when usually the real solution to the problem is thankfulness for what we already possess. Not having the ease of accessibility at one's fingertips along the trail created a heightened awareness of and appreciation for even the smallest provision.

Shelters

About a day's hike apart on the whole trail are small, three-sided lean-tos that generally resemble small rustic cabins. Though most hikers carry a tent or tarp, many still plan their daily walk shelter to shelter. Shelters are a place to prepare for the next day's journey, excellent for company and even sleep when not being entertained by an improvisational choir of snorers. Tents are better for sound sleeping, and especially conducive to oversleeping when waking to a rainy morning. There are few things more luxurious on the trail than sleeping with the rain softly pattering on the walls of a leak-proof tent.

Towards the end of a long day, especially in the cold or in a storm, it is easy for one's sense of distance to be skewed by weariness or shattering raindrops. Growing anticipation of drawing near day's end was sometimes overtaken by suspicion of overshooting what is often an obscurely marked side trail leading to the shelter. This typically progressed to dread that it might actually be several more miles before a determination could even be made that one was no longer walking *to*, but actually away *from* the shelter—and a desperately needed dinner and night's rest. What relief when a dully glimmering tin roof would suddenly appear through the mosaic of leaves. The otherwise dark and drafty structures could not have seemed more like home than at such times.

On the trail, there is no time to dwell in the past. It requires constant forward movement, which in of itself has a way of washing away the regret of days gone by. Certain situations in life are only intended to be shelters for a time, but need to be moved away from in due time in order to continue progressing on one's life path.

Soul Clothing

The trail has many ways of reminding the hiker that the body is clothing for the soul, but it is not the person. As with other exerting sports, thru-hiking at times requires the hiker to distinguish the body as entirely apart from the self, allowing it to be viewed as a kind of sophisticated transport for the metaphysical, all the way to the next enormous meal in town.

On a long uphill push, the gradual rising and dispersion of heat generated by the effort reveals the body as a kind of walking furnace: where there is heat, there is life. This was reinforced at other times, such as waking up too cold to sleep in the middle of the night and forcing down a snack in order to raise one's caloric level just to be able to get back to sleep; or stopping to pull on cumbersome raingear to avoid the threat of hypothermia when it would be easier and more comfortable to just walk in the rain.

When natural law is violated, setbacks or even catastrophe can result. When the boundaries the body is created to work within are not respected, the result is discomfort, pain, or even death. Deciding to leave a maintained path and bushwhack without map or compass inevitably results to wandering and waste. The trail is the safest and most efficient way to get where we are going. It is not hard to follow, though it takes determination to keep to it.

Sometimes we get off the path without meaning to: the momentum of our flesh can carry us one way when we actually prefer to go another.

Storms had taken the bridge out at Laurel Fork gorge in Tennessee, requiring hikers to step across the upper part of the falls where the water sluiced over a broad embankment, just wide enough to cross in relative safety aided by a rope secured on either side of the falls. A log ladder just south of the falls crossing led down a sheer vertical drop. The logs were muddy and slippery, and after carefully negotiating the descent, I stepped over to the very edge of the falls where the water was not moving fast and bent down to wash the mud off of my hands before stepping over to the rope to cross.

Sickeningly and without warning, my boots instantly began to slip sideways directly toward the first ledge where the roaring falls dropped steeply some indeterminate distance. The hiker directly behind me whom I had just helped down the ladder stood at the edge, reaching as far as she could from safe footing and screamed for me to grab her hand. I shouted something about not wanting to pull her over the falls even as my heart dropped into my stomach: there was nothing to hold on to, no recourse, no stopping. As I did my best to prepare for broken bones—or worse—miraculously, my feet suddenly stopped moving. Inching back from the danger onto dry, secure ground, my heart pounding, I was amazed and relieved to find myself intact. Another "second" chance.

Lessons Learned in Stone

My worst spills on the trail took place when I was barely moving or at a complete standstill. The times it seems I should have fallen when literally running down the trail for a change of pace, I never fell: proof once more that simply maintaining momentum is perhaps more crucial for stability than excessive care about one's footing.

Falling on a long hike is not only probable, it is inevitable. My first good spill was in the Smokies.[2] I was moving along nonchalantly when a slight sound in the trees diverted my attention just long enough to take my focus off the path. The next thing I knew, I was lying in it, head at the north end, on a slight decline. No sooner had I made the unexpected transition from vertical to horizontal than I realized the burden on my back enforced an involuntary repose, despite my best attempts to resume upright status.

---

[2]   Not that it is particularly relevant where it happened, but may be interesting that it took me that long from the beginning of the trail to have a good spill. I knew hikers who admitted to falling every day, some even several times a day, and I rather admired their cavalier approach in contrast to my own perhaps overstudied carefulness.

Thankfully, several friends were soon to come around the bend. "Look, a beached whale!"[3]

I lay on the ground laughing, feeling like a beetle and identifing with the main character in Kafka's *Metamorphosis*. The more I struggled to stand up, the harder I laughed as my friends looked on, amused. Realizing I wasn't going anywhere as long as the pack was attached, I unstrapped the weight pinning me to the ground, and my friends helped me to my feet. Never had I felt so consummately inept, yet somehow, not even the slightest bit embarrassed.

Our burdens can dictate not only how effective we are on our feet, but how we respond when we fall. Often our perception of the load we carry may be greater than the load itself. And how we deal with it can dictate how quickly we resume our path. We are most likely to stumble when we are tired. Even so, the space between a fall and getting back up on our feet can be a much needed rest. The friends who can laugh with us because they know us as we really are, and will wait to pull us back up to our feet when we miss the mark can make all the difference at such times.

The law of stone is wordlessly spoken in its unrelenting givelessness. It is a good surface for walking: it is supportive. But it is not a pleasant surface for falling. The same quality that makes stone supportive is what causes pain when met with flesh and bone. Law was first given inscribed on stone tablets; and like the law of gravity, its unrelenting nature supports us only as long as we walk according to its inflexibility. But when we fall, it hurts and even harms. Sometimes we stumble because we aren't paying attention, but most times, no one sets out with intentions to fall. Grace alone breaks the fall and helps us to our feet again. With it comes an invitation to leave the place of regret and live from the place of possibility; to unstrap our burden, reposition it manageably and again make progress.

---

[3] Before leaving for Georgia, a coworker had identified a website for schoolchildren that featured the migrational swim of a humpback whale nicknamed "Mogo" whose progress was tracked and detailed online by means of a radio transmitter attached to the whale. My coworker joked that he and our other colleagues should seize an opportunity to affix a radio transmitter collar some night when I was working late and falling asleep in front of the computer, in order to remotely enjoy the epic challenges of my hike from the comfort of their armchairs. Somehow, the name "Mogo" stuck. Over time, one's trail name takes on the character of the hike and eventually carries the weight of one's given name.

Coastal Pennsylvania

For many days before reaching Pennsylvania, we were warned in person, by guidebook and even in balladry of the state's claim to fame: mile after laborious mile of ankle-turning rocks. The first days out of New Jersey were rockier than portions of the trail further south, but certainly did not seem to warrant writing or singing about. We assumed we had seen the worst, and made many disdainful remarks about all the warnings of people and print that had induced such fear. But as the terrain gradually grew rockier, harsher, and crushingly slower, we had to swallow our words. We were now in the midst of the balancing act which was southern Pennsylvania.

Previously, it had seemed steep inclines and descents were the most challenging to navigate; but while the rocky sections were flat, they were anything but easy. The otherwise level path had been displaced by a motionless river of sharply pointed rocks. The constant attention required simply to walk and remain upright was exhausting. Applying intense focus to something so painfully mundane yet necessary was remarkably draining but the alternative was not at all pleasant.

The rocks would have been ideal if we were albatrosses dropping clams out of the sky in order to eat dinner. But there were no clams and we weren't going to turn into albatrosses anytime soon. Yet, oddly enough, some former coworkers living nearby came out for a brief camp out and hike, promising to bring dinner. To our surprise, dinner turned out to be a clambake, my first, which takes something for a New Englander to admit in the middle of the Pennsylvania woods. The other irony of the visit was that the coworker who was least convinced of the joys of thru-hiking spent a day traversing one the most vicious stretches of trail. He probably hung up his hiking boots for good afterwards.

Eventually, the rocks tapered off even as they had begun. We walked the hard-tamped soil with a greater appreciation for a smooth path than ever before. Rocky places can ultimately invoke a sense of gratitude that the whole trail was not that way, and for not coming out the other side sustaining any more repercussions from the unforgiving ground than feet sore from the constant pounding. Thankfulness generally leads to trust. If we don't trust things will get better, we complain, we doubt, and are tempted to quit. However, if we are confident something or Someone will come through for us, we wait for it even as we actively persevere, even when it feels like futility in the moment. And as we wait, we rest and are strengthened.

Caught

There is a big difference between something taking place and something taking hold.

One cold morning in the early days of the hike, after several days of rain and fog, the drippy mist seemed heavier, colder and inescapably nearer than all the other days combined. For the first time since stepping foot on the trail, I felt stuck. Simply walking away from the experience was not an option, at least not without slogging for many miles through the same wind and rain, to a yet-as-undetermined end. A sense of claustrophobia began to descend while tree limbs overhead dripped icy rain, the trail a thin muddy line scribbling its way north an indeterminate distance. I decided my only recourse was a break.

Somehow, it suddenly seemed intuitive that nothing less than auditory words would shatter the ominous silence of the woods that added to my admittedly irrational fear. Suspending my natural resistance to such measures, I spoke up. "What you need now is a good break. Slow down, take your pack off, get some snacks out, you'll be just fine." Slinging my pack to the ground, the dropping of its weight felt like a spring-released catch suddenly undone. I pulled a bag of snacks out of the top-hatch of my pack and watched as bright orange bits of cheese crackers sprinkled down, contrasting with the dark, wet ground, as out of place as the sound of spoken words in the silence. I reassured myself I was going to be just fine; that there was really nothing to be anxious about.

By the time the crackers were gone, I no longer felt the need to flee. It was as if the fear-filled interval had never happened. But I was amused such measures had been necessary to take the next step.

It was the beginning of release from the sense of being perpetually held hostage by circumstances over which I had no control. While not every moment that presents itself is pleasant, there is always freedom to choose one's response.

From that point on, the Appalachian Trail was home, was food and bread, pillow and blanket, raw sustenance, pure equilibrium. It was a cure for complacency and the great refuter of excuses to not follow a path of adventure.

All things bright and beautiful,
All creatures great and small,
All things wise and wonderful,
The Lord God made them all.

Cecil F. Alexander

three | Creatures and Critter Getters

Keeping company on the trail for months on end with plants and animals can have the long-term effect of reviving a soul made dusty and dry by immersion in an overly complex society that finds security and meaning in man-made devices which ultimately insulate us from creation and make us dependent on things we don't need. On the trail, life is defined in much simpler and more life-giving terms, and allows us time to be in touch with thoughts, feelings, dreams and desires. To be at the mercy of creation does have its limits, however.

Within the first twenty-five miles of the trail, raw weather drove a small group of us to seek more familiar creature comforts than what our backpacks could possibly contain. We decided to take our first break from the woods at the next trailhead.

A bit chagrined about pulling off-trail after such a short stint, there was nevertheless growing agreement that slogging through rain and mud for hours at a time was not particularly brilliant. There was nowhere to adequately dry soggy gear, temperatures were dipping down into the twenties, and the relentless inner dialogue kept up an insistent refrain: "What were we *thinking*?"

As we stood at the roadside with thumbs sheepishly extended, to our surprise, it was only minutes before a small pickup pulled off to the side of the road. Without so much as rolling down the window, the driver pointed behind him to the truck bed. We laughed at what was painted on the side of the truck as we clambered over the sides, finding ourselves perched precariously on top of old tires and whatever else he was hauling. After a short, cold ride into town, the truck zoomed away and we all agreed that a more appropriate vehicle could not have picked us up: "The Critter Getter." The trail has a way of reminding even the most confident hiker where they stand as a limited creation.

The driver took us to a small general store where we placed a call to some local cabins for rent. During the long, cold wait for our ride, we wandered in and out of the store for warmth, garnering a richer and more complete snack assortment with each visit, much to the delight of the cheerful shopkeepers.

Finally, our ride arrived. There were more hikers than seats and seat belts in the SUV as we careened at swift speeds piled two hikers deep along sharply switchbacked roads. To suddenly find oneself in a stranger's vehicle moving at speeds well in excess of the two to three miles an hour a hiker averages is more of an adjustment than it might seem; let alone with a driver who keeps turning around to ask questions, listening to passengers' responses with a generously long gaze, one hand on the wheel, the other clutching a bottle wrapped in a brown paper bag. Our driver cheerfully described the terrain that I was becoming convinced we would know all too intimately before the drive was over, watching the ground drop far below, hairpin after sharp hairpin turn. My anxiousness reached a pitch and then could go no further, not unlike my head jammed nearly sideways against the roof of the car. I concluded that there was nothing to be done but endure it, and hopefully survive. From there, the ride went from fearful to slightly exhilarating to just plain silly as I pondered the ironies of existence, twirling like leaves in an updraft up and around mountain peaks.

We finally made it to the lodge, and to our even greater astonishment than arriving at all, found it full of familiar faces. Clearly, we were not the only ones with the wherewithal to realize that it was not reprehensible to pull off the trail long enough to get wet gear and nerves back on track, even if mid-ride, it seemed we had merely traded one form of intolerable for another.

Stepping into our cabin after the important business of ordering pizza, within short order, a web of thin nylon rope crisscrossed the room, tied down at every available door knob, drawer pull and chair leg. If the fact that the prime real estate of the room was now taken up with soggy wet gear was a challenge, nothing could have prepared us for the stench of six people's woefully wet socks and assorted gear drip-drying in concert. Surveying all the tents hanging in angles around the room, someone said: "Yep, good idea to dry 'em out before they started growing potatoes."

Hummingbird

A few weeks before I left for Georgia, a close friend with powerful gifts of perception had a strong sense that a profoundly new level of healing was coming to me in five months' time. I questioned such explicit foreknowledge, yet hoped it was true without necessarily believing it would come to pass.

I didn't think much more about it until a few weeks into the hike after arriving at Kincora, a favorite hostel owned and operated by several of the kindest people of any established wayside along the trail. The hostel had a tiny telephone room with a large window looking out into the woods. In the midst of a call home, conversation turned to some of issues I had unwittingly come to the trail to face, naturally rising to consciousness by almost limitless distraction-free hours hiking.[4]

I found myself dubiously recounting my friend's prophetic word about a new measure of healing allegedly on its way as I stared through the window into the dense stand of hardwoods beyond. Scarcely had the words been uttered before a hummingbird suddenly zipped into center view, mere inches from my astonished gaze on the other side of the glass. With furiously beating wings, this small living jewel hovered for several moments before zooming away as quickly as it had come. I could not explain it, but chose to take it as confirmation that good was on its way.[5]

Snakes in Swimming Holes

A wide, inviting boulder big enough for two or three sat in the sunlight just on the north side of the River Tye at one end of a long suspension footbridge. I half expected to see a large, squat troll guarding the bridge, and decided if one appeared we could probably bribe him with Snickers, squashed oatmeal cream pie cookies or something else from the typical hiker snack arsenal.

Deciding to take advantage of the waterfront vista for lunch, the dock-like boulder became the site for a hiker picnic. Angled sunlight rippled in bright

---

[4] While I would not have traded this experience of being completely shut off from the distraction of phone, internet or iPod along the trail, especially in the early days of the walk, "back when I was a thru-hiker" I was happy to borrow a walkman and a hiking partner's mix tape by the time I reached Pennsylvania.

[5] The third month on the trail, my friend's word indeed came to pass. It is a story I love to share, but like others, it is one to be told in person.

bands through the clear water to the rocky bottom, beckoning a quick bathe. Water sources are plentiful along most portions of the trail, but are not always deep enough to take a dip. After a leisurely swim, we went on our way much refreshed. That night after some other hikers caught up with us, one exclaimed: "I had the worst experience at the Tye today! I was sitting just minding my own business having a lunch by the river when a water snake suddenly appeared in the water, turned its head like a periscope and began swimming straight for me!" It was my first time hearing that water snakes in the region are not poisonous but nevertheless aggressive and will bite when threatened. I had to laugh at my lingering soak in the river, ignorant of what was possibly heading my way unseen. But perhaps I would have enjoyed the rare opportunity for a trailside dip anyway, even knowing the potential of a reptilian interruption. Wise choices are probably best made in the tension between the known and the unknown—but ultimately, wisdom calls for *the innocence of a dove, and shrewd eyes of a serpent.*[6]

Box Turtle

Hiking up a small knoll one day, my pace was arrested by the presence of orange and black armor: a box turtle gracing the path. I marveled at this being's careful, almost reflective movements and wondered if it ever felt discouraged to move so slowly in the context of so many other swift and able-bodied creatures. But there seemed to be a secret to its perfection. Its personal blueprint required very small, very slow paces, seemingly laborious and studied, as if each step was its first. If this miniature dinosaur was discontent with the parameters of its being and aspired to scamper like a squirrel, it would be humorously futile. Being ponderous by nature suggests thoughtfulness, with time for contemplation of things like the shingles of the sky overhead, how they hold in place without a single nail.

No extraneous creatures exist in the kingdom of creation; all reveal different facets of wisdom through a myriad of unique shapes and dispositions. Without a revelation of each, our knowledge is partial, incomplete.

Old Man Bird

Another ordinary day on the trail walking alone for hours, I suddenly had the distinct sensation of being watched. I paused, looked all around, but there was no one in sight, not a solitary noise to betray a soul; only a small breeze

[6]   Matthew 10:16

moving in the trees, the leaves clasping hands with one another, trembling as it passed.

I found myself stepping back a few paces on the trail, and then it caught my eye: a tiny fledgling, not more than an inch and a half in stature, quietly occupying a twig reaching in my direction. Steady black eyes peered unwaveringly back at me with solemn intensity, small tufts of silky-looking feathers protruding from either side of its head and disproportionately large beak. He resembled a little balding old man missing his choppers.

With not so much as a sound or gesture, we gazed sharply at one another, acutely aware of the otherness of each. A reverence welled up within at this tiny creature, so perfectly formed, so rapturously present and almost camouflaged on that spare twig, so stalwart in spite of overwhelming vulnerability. He was a comically fierce little soul; amazing to think of that tiny heart pumping with deliberation all the life-blood he had within; born with the freedom of wings so tightly clasping its little body, like a seed not fully germinated.

We gazed at each other a moment longer before I moved on down the trail. Somehow, each ensuing step fell differently into the path, altered because of my encounter with this little being, so tiny of stature yet huge in presence.

As I walked, I imagined him saying had he been able: "You humans think you know a lot, but if you only knew what I know. I have nothing to prove, I only exist to be, and in my being, I honor my Creator because it was by masterful intent that I am here. Don't think yourself too insignificant, neither believe yourself to be too important: we all fill a unique space, with exquisitely designed characteristics, set on this wandering star to gaze back into the eyes of the One whose eyes are intently upon us, who delights in our presence and even in our process, and is funnier, more loving and more present than you could possibly imagine. And here we two are, brimming with life for this brief moment we've been aligned to share: so ephemeral, yet filled with all the beauty and all the meaning a moment could hold."

There is a quiet glory all around us, and it does not take a mystic or saint to see, it only takes a moment, a choice to notice, to be willing to slow down and allow for sacred interruptions; to live fully this short day on the way to the grave and what lays beyond.

We are all pilgrims on the same
journey but some pilgrims have
better road maps.

Nelson DeMille

four | Pilgrims and Other Characters

I had originally envisioned the thru-hike as a lonely sojourn: nothing but Creator, earth and sky with only occasional companionship on the pilgrimage. I had not anticipated there would be so many others working their way along the winding ribbon of land from the mountains of northern Georgia to the Maine wilderness. The trail was filled with some of the most fully alive souls I have ever known, and in towns along the way some of the kindest people eager to help us on our way. It was a great cure for cynicism about people's ability to be magnanimous, even to or especially on behalf of perfect strangers.[7]

The company of fellow adventurers soon became one of its greatest joys. The trail was our common thought, dream and language. Life on the trail had so little to do with life lived off the trail. It was a rare opportunity to essentially hit the reset button on life: a new name, new friends and society, a new occupation and definition of home; a place carried within.

Hikers tend to find in their fellow sojourners a hunger for experiencing life with abandon, unafraid to walk into the unknown and be presented with unnamed challenges. Hikers walk trusting to be guided to safety through the difficulties which are part of any meaningful path. There are few things sweeter than the meeting of minds and hearts of fellow travelers who companion the long way, bonded by the same enabling grace to get up and walk each day. While the trail broadly represents the perseverance to finish a certain course, it is the presence of others that strengthens each all the way to the goal.

---

[7] 'Trail angels' are usually unseen individuals who leave food and beverages for unsuspecting hikers at road crossings or who provide support in countless ways along the trail.

To be a thru-hiker is to be a person of faith, regardless of creed or religion. When reason suggests such a foolishly long walk should not even be attempted, the belief that it just may be possible fuels the journey. The typical long-distance hiker represents a passionate quest to not only answer deeper questions of existence, but to find a reason to celebrate meaningful moments all along the way.

Every hiker adds a unique color and texture to the trail, becoming part of its living, shifting beauty. It is a wild, open cathedral where the wind can move freely, and for once, civilized man is a guest in the domain of nature. A never-before-heard harmony is cultivated with each mile deeper into this undomesticated terrain, the path itself the one ordered line through the tangled mystery of the woods and all that it harbors.

An otherwise dark campsite is filled with warmth and light by the camaraderie of fellow sojourners spattered with the same mud, exerted by the same climbs and inspired by the same heights. Pure, unspoken understanding reigns regardless of race, age or creed. Hikers are almost normal folks, representing for the most part a fairly broad swath of humanity. But there are certain common denominators. Hikers like a good challenge, and are about the joys slung between feast and famine, slogging up and down rugged hills rain or shine whilst surviving blisters and sporting farmer's tans; the culinary austerity of chewing on often tasteless rehydrated food and its unmentionable side-effects; and a number of other details that while hardly endurable at the time, make for the best stories later.

One must believe in the journey before it can be successfully undertaken, and it remains a walk of faith to the end. A roving community of peaceful warriors, dirty outside, pure of motive inside, hikers for the most part are a hearty fellowship repelled by the empty rites of modern society. Happy to abandon for a time traditions about being proper, safe, or culturally relevant, overturning the tables of traditions like: wash your hands before eating. Don't get caught in the rain and stay out of mud puddles. Sleep indoors. Don't talk to strangers. Never hitchhike. Don't be seen publicly before making oneself presentable. Work nine to five till you're too old to enjoy what's left of your life. Do only what mainstream society says to be relevant and acceptable.

A thru-hiker is someone who thrives on a degree of mystery; is not afraid of any unknown quantity, or getting caught in the rain; who knows the balance between relying on self and relying on others to keep to the trail. Every activity has its saturation point, but little compares to the simple joy of splashing through mud puddles in a warm summer downpour, washing the effort of miles away.

The values and jurisdiction of the trail are peace, contemplation, and a somewhat reckless sort of volition to go through whatever the mighty Unknown dishes up, even if just to see what lies around the next bend. Hunted down by a sense of hope, awakening, and a great longing to grasp what had perhaps previously been thought an unattainable goal before the realization that it was always worth pursuing, regardless of the final outcome.

Rather than being compromised by the nomadic nature of the thru-hike, if anything, hiker community is strengthened by the changing nature of the days and the vulnerability that is a natural part of risking life and limb on the long way. Trail family ties are strong ones.

Trail Head

Waking up in the shelter with eight or ten other grubby hikers is a fine way to start the day. You notice your neighbor's seriously rumpled hair, intermittently squashed and standing straight on end, knowing that you are looking at a mirror. Every day is a chance to see yet another visual definition of "trail head."

In essence, it was a daily glimpse into a rare kind of freedom: the hike is about what lies beyond outward appearances. Few delights compare to being able to relate with others such leveled honesty, humility and humor.

And while the hiking costume varies somewhat person to person, there is a certain homogenization of personal effects which make the aspect of judging and comparing and stereotyping less possible than in other segments of society. On the trail, we are given a rare glimpse apart from the everyday outward show that people present. In so-called civilized society, we typically judge others based on occupation, personal style and sensibilities, but what if appearance were a non-factor? How would we relate? The trail enables us to see past superficialities and needless distinctions, and interact more directly with true persona. *Man looks on the outward appearance, but God looks on the heart.*[8]

---

[8]   I Samuel 16:7

Great fellowship is to be found in the idiosyncratic commonalities of the journey, far stronger than the obvious diversity of ages, backgrounds and lifestyles represented: the overriding connection trumped what might otherwise divide. People who seek connection with others based upon what ties us as human beings and are less concerned about differences are a great gift. The trail was a rare window into the possibility of relating to others in a more sincere way. For all its ups and downs, the trail itself is the great leveler, regardless of age, gender or life experience.

On the trail, most people set aside their given name for a season and adopt a trail name, which goes along with the experience of leaving "normal" life for a season. This new name may reflect some aspect of the person's character, appearance, or highlight a particular event on the trail. It is a nickname, an association that through the course of the hike, as strange as it may sound, becomes as real as one's birth name. A proverb of Solomon states that *a good name is better than fine perfume.* Good news for long-distance hikers and the aroma often associated.

Purists and Gracists

Sometimes the detour is the preferable path—we miss out on what we might have otherwise enjoyed trying to be overly exact.

Early into the thru-hike, conversation around the campfire often turned to comparisons with other hikers: what kind of gear they carried, how much weight, how far they had managed to walk in one day. The level of conviction expressed by proponents of the varying schools of thought was amusing to witness, so deep in the woods miles removed from the comparative civilization of modern society.

Some complained with ardent zeal about those who were "cheating" on the trail by taking alternate trails to get where they wanted to go. Occasionally, a side trail would loop around a portion of the trail or bypass it entirely. Sometimes an alternate trail was marked as a high-water route to take in the event of a flooded trailside stream. But regardless of the reason for a secondary trail's existence, reasons to take an alternate route are as varied as the hikers themselves, and there were always those who took it upon themselves to critique.

The term used in the hiking community for people who intend to walk past every white blaze painted on the entire trail is a 'purist.' I hadn't walked but one day when I was confronted with my first purist dilemma. The shelter area had two trails running into it, one on the north side, one on the south. Logic suggested that one trail lead in, one trail lead out. As I headed for the "exit" trail, someone pointed out that there was a span of perhaps twenty yards of Appalachian Trail between the access trails, and to not go back out the same way I came in would be to miss that portion. Not wanting to compromise my thru-hiker honor, I retraced my steps. Hiking partner Gollum later made the brilliant observation: "What about all the spaces between each footstep on the path? Are the purists intending to go back and fill in those, too?"

Several states later, a few of us arrived at a fork in the trail. According to the guidebook, what was now a side path leading to a waterfall had once been the Appalachian Trail footpath; it had later been rerouted over a particularly scenic ridgeline. We decided that when given the choice of a view or waterfall on a hot summer day, a waterfall prevailed. Still, having kept to the purist's credo up to that point, we felt somewhat reprobate as we knowingly left the well-trodden path for the less-traveled blue-blazed trail. The path led to yet an even narrower side trail and directly to the stepped waterfalls cascading into deep, clear pools. A hasty liberation of overworked feet from hot boots and clinging socks later, we dove into the pools again and again, laughing, shouting and gasping for breath in the bracingly cold water, more than satisfied with our decision to take the trail less traveled. *Do not be overrighteous, neither be overwise—why destroy yourself? Do not be overwicked, and do not be a fool—why die before your time? It is good to grasp the one and not let go of the other.*[9]

Another traditional mindset on the trail is that in order to make any progress, the long-distance hiker must rise and hit the trail just before dawn, and arrive at camp before dark. Other hikers however are more event than time oriented, preferring to sleep in, perhaps having paused to watch a beautiful sunset the night before, or enjoyed the mystery of a night hike, especially beautiful when the moon is bright. In the heat of summer, it was wisdom to make as many miles in the cool of the day as possible; but in reality, both approaches result in covering the same amount of miles.

If there is any virtue in rising early or rising late, it lies more within the individual remaining true to their own walk, than just simple adherence to a social tradition or superficial understanding of how it is "supposed" to be done.

---

[9] Ecclesiastes 7:16

Fire in the Rain

Even circumstances that seem insurmountable can have an open door. The past can be remembered and the future can be written by the limitless freedom to choose one's attitude to any situation in the present.

There were days and nights when the cold seemed to be an entity to contend with. When the day's walking was done, the reality of it was confronted like the death we are all trying to avoid. The company of others not only made it bearable, but seemed as crucial to well-being as physical protection from the elements.

Gooch Gap shelter was small, every inch of floor spread with gear and the few hikers fortunate enough to make it in before the little lean-to reached capacity. Night was falling, and with it, rain. We reluctantly walked away from the shelter but soon arrived at a small clearing, just the right size for our four tents. Two of our crew were expert fire makers, and despite the weather, built a bonfire that was hot enough to dry the clothes we were wearing—even in the rain. A curious juxtaposition of elements and attitudes. We stayed up talking and joking late into the night, enjoying what had turned out to be not only a tolerable evening but a most memorable one. To think what we would have missed had we slept in the crowded shelter and the slightly more substantial creature comforts it would have afforded. A potentially miserable evening was turned around by the fire of indefatigable spirits fully present to the moment, finding shelter more in the company of each other than just under a roof.

Loaves and Fishes

"Trail magic" by definition usually happens when least expected, is most needed, or sometimes even just when wanted, often surpassing in quality what was desired to begin with.

Just weeks from the trail's southern terminus, just as everyone was settling in for the night, two hikers ran into the shelter area laughing uncontrollably. They had just experienced their first trailside miracle, and were nearly bursting to tell the story.

On a quest earlier in the afternoon for a quick snack food resupply, they had hitched a ride to a nearby campground. By the time they arrived, the store was already closed for the day, apparently still on an off-peak-season schedule.

Finding a ride while the sun was still shining on the narrow, switchbacked roads of the remote Georgia mountains was challenging enough, but with sundown and a closed store, the hikers were beginning to panic about the likelihood of getting back to the trailhead. As they stood feeling helpless and a little foolish at the side of road hoping for a ride that didn't seem to be coming, a local fisherman happened by. Not only did he drive them back to the trailhead, but after learning they were short on food supplies, he offered a few cleaned trout filets. While the rest of us ate rehydrated noodles for dinner, they feasted on pan-fried trout and were known from that point on as "Loaves" and "Fishes."

Some weeks later, a group of us had just left town after a zero[10] and a resupply. Unbeknownst to the rest of us, one hiker had forgotten to buy fuel for his camp stove. As dehydrated food makes for much of the hiker's diet and requires boiled water to reconstitute, fuel is essential. Typically, there is not extra for sharing, as both gear and supplies are kept to minimal and precise measurements with just enough to make it to the next resupply point. By the time he realized his oversight, we were too far into the woods to turn back.

Yet just about a mile or two later, we hiked into a small, otherwise pristine clearing and there next to a log at the side of the trail sat a small can of white gas, almost looking like it had been staged. There was no evidence of a recent campout and no other gear or supplies left behind. It wasn't even the commonly used generic fuel purchased from a hardware store, but rather, a more expensive brand only available from an outfitter store—with just enough fuel to make it to the next town.

Cake Cop

After restocking at a local grocery store in a little town in Georgia, we were walking across the parking lot back to our hostel when a police car slowly started driving toward us and pulled up alongside. We looked quizzically at each other, trying to figure out what had attracted his attention beyond our slightly grubby appearance and inordinate number of bulging plastic bags; did we look like grocery robbers?

---

[10] 'Zero' is the term used for a day off the trail with no walking planned, usually accompanied by a phenomena known as 'hiker hobble,' the peculiar gait adopted by long-distance hikers when walking on pavement without a backpack after many long days and miles carrying much weight.

We didn't have long to ponder the mystery. The cruiser stopped and out climbed an imposingly large policeman with just one question: "Do you like cake?"

We nodded compliantly and not a little enthusiastically, watching in bewildered silence as he popped the trunk: completely full of cakes. Pausing just for a moment to pick out the perfect one for the occasion, he triumphantly produced a chocolate cake studded with cookies, explaining that the grocery store regularly gave him day-old cakes. We were happy to help with the surplus problem.

Snow Angels

Our third morning in the Smokies, we awoke to a thick blanket of snow, the first real accumulation since starting the trail. As tempting as it was to linger in the shelter with the others choosing a slower start to the morning, it happened to be the day two of our hiking partners had arranged to meet with out of state friends at a nearby trailhead. With the path completely obscured under the newly fallen snow, it was clear our meet-up was going to be delayed.[11] We thought about splitting into two groups and trying to head the friends off at a different trailhead, just in case they anticipated a change in our exit strategy.

As we weighed the options, three hikers out camping for the week and wedged in with all the thru-hikers were listening as we discussed our dilemma. As we deliberated, one spoke up. "Hey, if y'all want to take our truck, it's parked at the next trailhead; keys are on the front wheel. You could drive to Newfound Gap and be there even before your friends arrive. We'll end our hike there instead. Just leave the keys back on the front wheel. Oh, and by the way, there's fifty dollars cash in the glove box with our drivers licenses." They weren't offering it; just letting us know they knew it was there. I was not the only one of our group from the city; this was unprecedented. Yet, it turned out to be the headwaters of many such instances along the trail that we were completely overwhelmed by the kindness, generosity and extended trust of total strangers.

---

[11] This was in the days when hikers carrying cell phones were perceived as a nuisance.

Grannie Annie

The first person to walk the entire Appalachian Trail end to end celebrated the fiftieth anniversary of his thru-hike by retracing his steps. At seventy-nine years of age and averaging twenty miles a day, he started the trail weeks after I began, finished weeks before I ended. Earl Shaffer was exceptional in many respects, but advanced years might have been the least of it. I met many people realizing their dream to thru-hike after retirement; most of them, like Earl, planned ambitious daily miles. Perceptions of age and limitation shift radically in the presence of those who seem to have forgotten or perhaps have never been told that after a certain age you can't hike—much less for six months at a time. When I meet people who express interest in hiking but give the well-worn line of defense "if I were your age," I like to tell them about Grannie Annie.

Hauling weary bones up a steep ascent one afternoon in Georgia, just days from the head of the trail, I caught up with a lanky elderly woman resting at the side of the trail, pure white hair curled into a bun, her deeply tanned face swagged in wrinkles. Pausing for a much-needed break, I said hello, asked how her day was going. "Terrible!" she said. "My daughter wants to go seventeen miles today, and I think I can only make fourteen!" For those not familiar with the Appalachian Trail through northern Georgia, it is no stroll through the park. Steep, seemingly endless ascents stretch on until finally approaching what only appears to be the summit, followed by many more "false" summits before reaching the top, an all too brief respite on the closest thing to level ground before the steep descent to the next gap, only to do it all over again, and again . . . and again. Ten miles is quite a full day in such terrain, so early in the conditioning stage. If Grannie Annie had been half her age, I would have been impressed. She was seventy-two.

Don't Judge a Man by His Raft

There was a hiker who joined our ranks early on who was missing all of his teeth. He muttered to himself as he hiked, and his responses to questions such as "how far is the shelter" or "where is the next water source" seemed to be in an obscure dialect that few could understand. We were all a little wary of him at first. But thru-hikers by nature band together for solidarity despite differences, and there were enough indicators as time went on that he was as serious a backpacker as the rest of us, despite his less-than-conventional appearance, even by thru-hiking standards.

The shelter area at Blue Mountain afforded us our first night seeing a sunset on the trail, one of the few viewable from a shelter. In the waning temperatures as the sun went down, everyone set about gathering wood dry enough for a fire, challenging after much rainfall. As we struggled to get the shreds of damp kindling to ignite, this particular hiker trudged off into the woods and soon emerged dragging a tree limb about a dozen feet in length which turned out to be dead, dry and very ready to burn.

He snapped it up into campfire-sized pieces, and soon we were warmed by bright blazing flames. After that bit of genius, he amused and confused us again by changing into a pair of enormous red down slippers that looked like giant baby booties. We might have been laughing at the time, but the last laugh was on us, shivering in our socks and athletic sandals on the frozen ground. Still, I found this choice in foot gear exceedingly odd until sometime later found them for sale in an outfitter store and saw they were indeed designed for outdoor use.

As night fell and the hissing of camp stoves ceased, we began to prepare for sleep in the shelter. This same hiker began to inflate an enormous yellow pool lounge; not exactly the expedition-quality sleeping gear the rest of us had. But as he lay back into his pool lounge with a loud satisfied sigh while the rest of us struggled to get comfortable on our expensive, wafer-thin hiking pads, I wondered who was really the wiser of the bunch.

Shelter Orphans

Any journey requires courage and focus to finish through unpredictable hurdles and hang-ups, the commitment to walk through whatever the weather, regardless if snow, sleet, rain or hail. Backtracking is avoided at all costs on the trail; nonetheless, at certain times it is necessary for ultimate forward movement. When events cycle and circumstances repeat, something may be trying to get our attention; we can notice or choose to ignore.

On a cold and rainy day's walk out of Hot Springs, North Carolina, we arrived at the shelter area set in a field and surrounded by a shallow moat of puddles and mud. The hikers who had arrived ahead of us and were already settled into the relatively dry space greeted us with smug smiles as we stood soaking in the downpour, inquiring as to nearby tent sites as there was no adequate space in view. The less-than-empathetic attitudes of these fellow hikers seemed a perfect reflection of the dreary day. Others were setting up tents in the mud under the dripping eaves of the shelter. Several of us decided to hike on in search of a better campsite, if there even was such a thing to be found in the heavily puddled terrain.

Among us was a retired military man who hiked on a few yards ahead of me, loudly exclaiming his dissatisfaction with the situation to no one in particular. I echoed the sentiments, but opted for resilience with what shreds of resolve I possessed: the cold, rain, weariness, and lack of a desirable campsite were bad enough.

Within a short distance and a turn in the trail, I came across a bewildering sight. A small group of hikers were nonchalantly standing at the edge of the trail, talking, laughing and sharing snacks, apparently oblivious to the weather. One smiled as I approached and asked how I was, his face shining through the rain as if he stood in a sunbeam.

For a moment I questioned my faculties: were we still caught in a downpour or had too many hours of morbid introspection done a number on my cognitive abilities? Delighted not only by how inconsequential the rain was to these hikers but more so how it had actually been seized for joy, I decided that moment I wanted to be more than neutral about the situation. To meet it not just with tolerance, but even with hilarity. What was there to lose? Only a dismal experience.

I hiked on with lighter spirits, glad for a renewed mindset, but campsite prospects were still bleak.

The guidebook had highlighted a small country store a short walk east of the trailhead at the next road crossing. It didn't take long to find refuge inside the tiny store, already occupied by the ex-marine who was entirely pleasant under a dry roof. In a short while, the merry rain people arrived. The marine decided enough was enough and would book a motel in Hot Springs for the night. We were all invited along; the room was on him. The shopkeeper, obviously used to such impromptu gatherings, patiently looked on as we talked through what to do while warming ourselves at a large electric heater in the middle of the store. After some discussion about the logic of backtrack when we were all actually headed north, we decided to accept the offer.

Hitching a ride back into town, we ended up renting a cabin at a campground not far from where our day had originally started. To add to the celebration, we visited the town's natural hot spring-fed tubs for an exceedingly more intentional and agreeable soak than the one we'd been caught in all day. We weren't regretting "no room at the inn" anymore. Sweet vindication! Three steps forward, two steps back is sometimes the only way to progress.

The Heaviest Weight in Your Pack

Economy of action, weight and the calibration of comfort with the lightest load possible is the thru-hiker's ongoing quest. At the beginning of the trail, any lack of backpacking experience is tempered by zeal and well-meaning attempts to plan for the unexpected; but the trail itself ultimately arbitrates what to keep and what to let go. Too much and weight becomes a liability; too little and a necessary baseline of comfort and safety is at risk. Comfort however shows up in different ways on the trail: a well-broken-in pair of boots. Reliable walking sticks. Cheerful companions.

Regardless of the company kept, conditions of the path, hiking experience or lack thereof, the trail requires us to let go of what is too heavy to carry. Sometimes in the attempt to bear ongoing burdens, our progress becomes unnecessarily slow and difficult. We find ourselves unable to walk our intended path unhindered; not because we lack desire or courage, but simply because we are carrying more than we can bear alone. We can even be prevented from finishing our course when we carry what we do not need.

The Walasi-Yi Center flanks the trail at Neels Gap in Georgia, just enough miles in for aspiring northbound thru-hikers to have had the first real taste of what it will take to walk all the way to Maine. Essential gear for sale and proprietors dedicated to consulting with shell-shocked hikers stumbling in for aid made it a strategic stop. My pack had been causing back pain, the last thing a long-distance hiker needs or wants. Even fully loaded, the backpack had been an optimal fit for the first few days, but had somehow worked itself into the need of a few expert adjustments I was not in a position to make myself. I had spent miles walking down the trail tugging straps and load lifters and pulling the pack off and putting it back on again, but something just wasn't right.

Surveying the outfitter's pack selection, I was daunted at the thought of needing such an expensive piece of gear so early in the walk for a problem that seemed more than likely remediable. Expressing my concern to one of the storekeepers, they immediately offered to reload my pack for the most efficient distribution of weight, and gave me the option to send any extraneous gear home.

Whether the storekeeper had the wisdom to know it wasn't the time for me to become a minimalist or deemed my pack size and weight acceptable was never expressed; there was no judgment of my process. When I left the store, my pack had the same exact contents, but felt ten pounds lighter. I was amazed that merely redistributing the weight could make such a difference. The pack never bothered my back again; nevertheless, I continued to lighten my load more as time went on.

The help of those more experienced than we are is essential to a fulfilled journey.

Rush had walked half the trail the previous year. Marked by a contagious passion for the hike, he was a zealous proponent and practitioner of lightweight backpacking. Though he was a seasoned hiker when we met, I was surprised to learn that on his first backpacking trip, long before thru-hiking the Appalachian Trail, he laughed to tell me he not only had he packed a pillow, but he used it to conceal a weapon in the event that something should go wrong.[12] He had come a long way since then, as we all had. Nothing delighted him more than the company of others similarly abandoned to the journey, letting trailish rigor stamp out needless fluff and filler, leaving only that which was of substance behind. Some love *to* hike, some love *the* hike; he loved both. After some discussion, he offered his services as a gear guru, and while somewhat confident that my pack was as light and efficient as it needed to be, I accepted.

Emptying the entire contents of my pack in an idyllic clearing near a brook edged with wildflowers, two gear piles formed: necessities. Non-necessities. The non-necessity pile was rather large. I was insulted by this presumptive, drastic pruning of my gear: who was he to say what I needed and didn't need?

---

[12] Many people come to the trail afraid of who or what may be encountered, and decide that being armed is the only remedy. Working through this fear is perhaps some sort of backpacker's initiation. Several days into the hike, I was still paranoid about falling asleep in my tent, wishing I could post vigil at the same time. After all, I was unable to see any sylvan predators conspiring against hikers lying oblivious in nylon bubble targets. Every woodland sound seemed to filter through the thin tent wall as the movement of a stealthy interloper headed my direction. Midway through that first fretful night, I finally decided that even if I ended up as a headline in the closest town's daily after being some creature's midnight snack, until the dastardly event actually took place, I wasn't going to lose any more sleep. I have slept soundly in a tent ever since.

The clincher was when he seized my end-to-end guidebook, opened it up and without asking permission proceeded to tear it apart section by section. "You don't need to carry the entire guide with you at one time; take only the section you need and send the rest on up ahead as you need it." Shock and some form of admiration for such chutzpah trumped indignation at seeing my book so dismembered. Along with other weight-trimming suggestions, it turned out to be one of the best bits of advice I received early in the hike, and later made me laugh to think I was carrying fourteen state's worth of information all at once.

When I broached the topic of necessities from a philosophical angle, his response was as practical as his approach: he would carry the "extra" gear for one day. At the end of the day, he would return it, and I could decide for myself what I could and could not live without. Easily six pounds lighter the following day's hike, my energy level and happier condition of my feet spoke for themselves. I had already forgotten what gear I had been so convinced of needing, though I still had little clue of the difference between what I thought I needed and what was actually necessary. But I was open to change. This was the key, and one of the defining moments of my hike. Rush's assessment:

"The heaviest weight you're carrying in your pack is your fear."

Hiker Clown Room Routine

Walking out of the woods with a fellow traveler who wore a watch with the word **NOW** taped over the face, we came to a rest area along a busy highway with a gas station convenience store and small motor inn. A humble scene, nevertheless, with a nearby carnival of snack options, laundry and shower, such a site was a kind of paradise for hikers. There were no cars in the parking lot, but looking down the row, every room appeared occupied with the jovial, ragtag troupe of now consummately fit hikers; backpacks, boots and random piles of gear could be seen marking the doorways. In a tiny room that would have been considered small for two people were wall-to-wall sleeping pads, random piles of gear, a half-gallon of melting vanilla ice cream and a liter of warm root beer. Somehow, less than ideal conditions, the least of which being refrigeration, made the anomaly of a root beer float party all the more superb. It was a reflection of the perfect imperfection and genuine community spirit that leaps over impracticalities for a higher cause: bringing joy to each other.

A new awareness came that evening, sleeping with the motel door wide open, crammed in with six other hikers and a dog: outdoors now felt like indoors.

While it is difficult to describe the exact feeling, at some indiscernible point, after being fully immersed for enough hours out of doors, being outside begins to seem the more natural, comfortable place to be; and by contrast, inside begins to feel confining, limiting. In life off the trail, being outside is generally only a passage between events or activities usually occurring indoors. On the trail, the opposite is true: indoors becomes the temporary interval, nothing more than a transport to where the hiker seems to most belong: in the great out-of-doors.

Viewed from the highway when hitching a ride from any given trailhead to town, the tree-covered hills no longer appeared to be a trackless waste, but rather, a place of familiarity, even of welcome. Despite the extra weight of a new food supply fresh out of town, it was usually a great relief to step back onto the trail and take oneself back amongst the trees, and ever closer to the goal. The hills had truly become home.

There is an inexplicable joy in the freedom of carrying absolutely everything needed not only to survive but even to be comfortable on one's back. Along with such mobility, not having a grip on a day's events can be marvelously liberating. Freedom to walk, freedom to trust. As if we really know what any day lived anywhere will ultimately hold anyhow.

The only journey is the one within.

Rainer Maria Rilke

five | Solitude

Moving through the endless green tunnel of limb and leaf held in uncertain but beautiful austerity, I never dreamed that the hike would take me from my longing for solitude to a newly developed aversion for its excesses. Prior to the trail, I had never experienced the limit of needing to be alone. As a natural introvert, it seemed there was never enough time outside of work and social obligations to find time away to think and to rest. On the trail, the tables were turned. Walking alone for hours and not having means to quickly reach the voice of a friend created at times an almost suffocating sense of isolation. Walking deeper by the mile into remote territory only further served to compound the fact that no quick remedy existed to trailish seclusion. For perhaps the first time in my life, I experienced a loneliness that could not be avoided. I marveled that I was, in fact, a closet "gregarian."

Isolation and loneliness are difficult twins that nevertheless can leave behind the fruit of patient endurance when there is really no other choice but to get through it to the other side.

Many, many days I walked for long hours wishing for a good friend to talk to.[13] There was no real way to make plans to meet up with a fellow hiker. If friends had fallen into a different pace further back on the trail, messages could be relayed via other hikers or notes could be left in shelter logbooks. But there was still no way of knowing how far away someone might be—or even if they

---

[13] In 1998, virtually no one carried a cell phone; the idea was that we had come to the woods to be free of such tethers. One night within the first few weeks of the thru-hike, when someone tenting nearby could be overheard on their phone, another hiker yelled: "Turn that thing off!" It was the first and last time I encountered such an "indiscretion" along the trail; proof that times have changed quite a bit since then.

were still on the trail. If they were up ahead, the hope of connecting was even slimmer, or at least, less detectable.

Yet, I observed a strangely consistent phenomena: when the need to talk to someone was the most acute, or conversely, when someone else needed a listening ear or word of encouragement just as much as I did, unbeknownst to either of us, we would inevitably come alongside each other with words profoundly needed. Whether the message came in the form of life stories related, poems recited or songs sung, their delivery could not have been more meaningfully precise had a letter been posted from beyond. It was a perfect harmonizing of the spiritual with the natural; a mysterious yet cohesive mingling of wholly unplannable events with psychological and spiritual provision for the moment. Such encounters were uncanny, but equally undeniable, as if there were an agenda of events no less purposeful for being "random," written in a script of air molecules and water droplets.

It was hard to view these impromptu meetings as anything but divinely orchestrated. In a universe of profoundly complicated proportion, it is easy to feel like not much more than an insignificant particle. But to have thoughts only ever uttered in the heart addressed so specifically and in the most unlikely places and times awakened a newfound belief in a Creator's benevolent intersection in even the smallest of concerns.

I will never forget the sense of having stepped into the realm of greater possibilities on the day I longed to talk with a particular hiker I had not seen in weeks. Our conversations were always miles deep and seemed perpetually beginning. As I walked and struggled through the desire for connection that didn't seem possible, I uttered a simple prayer for my heart's need to be met, regardless of who was or was not there. I felt my sense of urgency dissolve into surrender, and I walked on in peace.

I hiked around another bend in the trail: and there, to my astonished delight, was my longed-for friend. Perched on a throne-sized rock, he grinned as I approached, as if awaiting my arrival at that exact moment, just minutes from releasing the need to connect again.

A common theme along the trail was that some desires are never fulfilled until they are completely let go. When we surrender a cherished longing, recognizing there are circumstances we cannot control to bring it into our keeping, only then are we in a position to receive what is longed for; and then, not as a thing earned, but as a gift given. And while enjoyed, still to be held loosely.

Considering the Source

When someone speaks as an authority on a topic they actually know little or nothing about, it is wise to weigh what they say against that fact. Ironically, the people most likely to speak discouragement about our ability to complete the entire trail were typically non-hikers off the trail, or if on the trail, only out for a brief stroll. I was amazed at how assertive the scoffing of perfect strangers could be to an honest answer of "all of it" in response to the question of how much of the trail we intended to cover. Early in the hike when there are many reasons to reinforce doubt, such discouraging words can be poison. Seasoned words at the right time are invaluable, and during challenging times, maybe even necessary to completing the course at all.

Far too many fledgling beginnings fail simply due to lack of belief and encouragement. Worse than hiking alone is being accompanied by someone discouraging along the path—whether they are in person, or via the memory and replaying of negative words spoken, no matter who or what the source. We can put unnecessary obstacles in our own path by believing the lie that we are not capable of achieving what we are in fact actually cut out to do. It can be far too easy to hang our best thoughts and intentions on the limited views of others. On or off the trail, it is crucial to learn how to filter the judgments of those who have not actually earned the right to speak into your life. Those who have gained that right have won it by unconditional love and support, sometimes even at their own expense. Trust such people, and let the negative perspectives of others who do not have your best interests at heart dissipate like toxins in a clean wind.

One of my bolder hiking companions, a tiny, vivacious middle-aged woman with a reputation for fearlessness had finally heard enough of such talk. At a trailhead in New England, a very large man made the mistake of questioning her ability to finish. As the story went, she fired back at him: "Do you think I've walked this trail all the way from Georgia to have someone who doesn't look like they could hike a mile tell me I'm not going to finish?"—all the while poking his sizable belly with her walking stick for emphasis. I am quite sure he thought twice before telling another thru-hiker that they weren't going to make it to Maine.

While the long way may require fighting off many hindrances that often come in the form of lack of moral support, it is ultimately eclipsed by the joy of completion. The integrity of effort all along the way is no less meaningful than accomplishing the goal, even as the surface of a rock is the same substance at its core. It is this perspective that lures us along through mud-sloshing alleys in the featureless corridors of a rain-soaked day, alone with one's thoughts, sodden gear and wet feet. If comfort were the only goal, we would lack the balance and sharpness the rigors of the trail both require and maintain.

When comfort is wearing thin, so is the veil separating us from what lies beyond the physical realm. Hidden in the simplicity of trail life is a kind of purity of intent which does not discriminate upon whom it rests, but to varying degrees may be concealed under many years of anxieties and distractions. The long hike allows for a shedding of these layers and a transcendence of the spirit, and with it, great freedom.

Commitment to the way when it seems the goal is in some inscrutably distant place can make one feel or be off balance. Some will ask why the fixation on something which seems more likely to fail than to succeed? Better to play it safe than risk the humiliation of failing. But once the path is completed, it doesn't matter what anyone thought or said. The naysayers will have to eat their words for breakfast, and if you are kind, you can offset their indigestion with a bit of counsel that they, too are capable of fulfilling their own dreams, whatever they may be, one humble step at a time.

Hike Your Own Hike

Being entirely removed from the constraints of society for a good long time allows the soul to stretch out, perhaps for the first time, in the freedom to simply *be*. Our minds have been battered by experiences resulting in judgments which have lined the spiritual path with so much junk that stepping over our own negative mindsets just to keep to the path can be wearying. But the trail mercifully holds no judgment. The inner eye constantly remains open to the process, and eagerly seeks its resolve.

"Hike your own hike" is a saying commonly heard along the trail. The way you plan and what gear you bring and how you labor up a mountain and why you place your feet on the rocks the way you do and how you respond when you fall and what you eat and why you prefer a tarp and how you pitch it and why you get up early or how much you love to night hike are no one's business but your own. Complete strangers may offer compelling opinions, but no one can tell you how to hike. The uniqueness of who we are, the way we walk and the choices we make as we go reveal the truth of who we are; and there is great joy when we are simply ourselves. Walking reveals that purpose just as hiking a trail reveals the path. If we are open to it, we will see that the Spirit communicates this to us in countless ways every day. A dramatic lesson is not always necessary, but sometimes it takes that to know where we stand, and from there, to see where we have been and where we have yet to go. In most instances, we do not need to be taught anything, only reminded of what we already know.

Speck Pond

While the experience of aloneness along the trail has its own value, having others alongside can make all the difference in staying the course. Standing in solidarity with those who want you to succeed as much as they do is powerful company. I did not doubt my ability to finish the trail, but it didn't seem like hubris to say I would follow through: I was driven by love of the process, and finishing the experience seemed a natural outcome.

My first and only major test of the will to keep to the hike came after an especially chilly night spent alone at an elevation above 4,000 feet in a drafty shelter by Speck Pond in New Hampshire, not far from the Maine border. Not many shelters are located at so high an altitude, and more rarely, on the edge of a wide expanse of water, a perfect runway for the wind. The shelter was built with its back to the view, presumably to reduce full expression of the wind's relentless pursuit across the pond all night. It was small compensation for the cold draft that nevertheless seemed to push its way through every fiber of every board in the shelter.

What would have been delightful on a hot summer night was almost unbearable at such an elevation late October in Maine. Laying my sleeping bag parallel with the back wall of the shelter to be as far from the wide entrance as possible, I climbed in and pulled the draw cord closely around my face. Wind battered the thin wooden walls of the shelter all night long, making attempts at sleep as futile as avoiding the cold that crept in closer by the hour.

Crawling out of my cocoon the next morning to find my nylon water bucket frozen over seemed one more cue that things were not going to get any easier, and ice water might be the least of it. I confronted the question that had not even crossed my mind until that instant. Could I really make it? Was I really equipped to finish? My backpack was already filled to capacity with winter gear, and not another piece of insulating clothing could possibly fit. How was I to stay warm? If I couldn't carry another ounce, how could I possibly shoulder colder weather?

As I broke camp, tears began to roll down my face as fear swiftly became a conclusion that I could not go on. The thought of leaving the trail was intolerable, but hiking north into Maine, north into cold and imminent winter seemed an impossibility.

I stepped back onto the trail with a heavy heart, a sense of my utter powerlessness to change circumstances which seemed immeasurably stronger than my ability to keep to the path. For the first time, the trail no longer felt like a path to joy. I plodded on with no other intention than to climb the next mountain and come down the other side to the gap with the road leading to a nearby town. I couldn't bring myself to think what might happen beyond a visit to the post office where some mail awaited.

As the elevation rose and the sun climbed higher in the sky, I cleared treeline and stepped onto a rocky dome near the summit, almost aglow with light. Feeling a deep, soaking warmth for the first time in several days, this time generated by the sun and not by my own effort, I pulled my pack off and sat in the comfort of the saturating rays.

Still feeling somewhat numb about what was yet pending, a day hiker suddenly bounded enthusiastically up the dome.[14] After a boisterous greeting, he asked me where I had hiked from. "Speck Pond." I replied. He looked at me with a "don't give me that crap" look and repeated, "No, where did your hike *begin*?" "Georgia." He face lit up triumphantly at indeed identifying me as a long-distance hiker. "What's wrong, you seem sad?" It was clear he couldn't understand how someone so close to victory could be so glum.

I described the previous night's sleeplessness and my fears about being able to stay the course despite not a previous moment's doubt nor waning desire. He listened well then raised an eyebrow. Looking at me intently, he said with conviction, "If I run into you after today and you tell me that you didn't finish, I'm going to kick your ass!" He offered to drive me into town if I wanted to wait at the trailhead while he finished summiting, and left the choice to me.

As I weighed the limited options, the angle of the sunlit rock was so severe and walls of the mountain pass in front of me so steep, the law of gravity seemed momentarily suspended. Somehow, the momentary illusion of a complete loss of the horizon was comforting: it echoed the bewildering mood of the day and seemed the perfect visual of literally looking at everything from a completely different perspective.

Having chosen the offer for a lift, I met my new ally in the parking lot at the trailhead. He drove nearly an hour out of his way on his one day off to a small

---

[14] A riddle heard along the trail: how can you tell a day hiker, section hiker and thru-hiker apart? A day hiker walks right past the M&M in the trail. The section hiker sees it, and packs it out. The thru-hiker eats it.

bed and breakfast frequented by hunters and hikers. He was as open, honest and down to earth as an old friend or close family member, and before driving away, gave me a huge hug with parting words of wisdom: "Not to worry. Call your family. Have some hot cocoa—you'll be fine!" As I internalized his advice and made my way to the door, I was immediately greeted by one of the owners whose first question was if I wanted a cup of coffee. I was told three other hikers had arrived the night before.

Steaming mug in hand, I ventured down the hallway and to my great surprise, likewise seeking refuge from the cold were fellow north bounders I had not seen since Virginia. Mentioning how cold, tired and shaky my resolve was for the first time since Georgia, the others said they had been feeling exactly the same way. The sense of solidarity was everything at that moment. We decided our meet-up was no coincidence and pledged to stick it out to the end.

The bitterest portion of a path can be made sweet by the presence of others.

Of Being Woven

The way is full of genuine sacrifice.
The thickets blocking your path are anything that keeps you from that, any fear that you may be broken into bits like a glass bottle.

This road demands courage and stamina, yet it's full of footprints!
Who are these companions? They are rungs in your ladder. Use them!

With company you quicken your ascent. You may be happy enough going along, but with others you'll get farther, and faster.

Someone who goes cheerfully by himself to the customs house to pay his traveler's tax will go even more lightheartedly when friends are with him.

Every prophet sought out companions. A wall standing alone is useless, but put three or four walls together and they'll support a roof and keep grain dry and safe.

When ink joins with a pen, then the blank paper can say something.
Rushes and reeds must be woven to be useful as a mat.
If they weren't interlaced; the wind would blow them away.

~Rumi

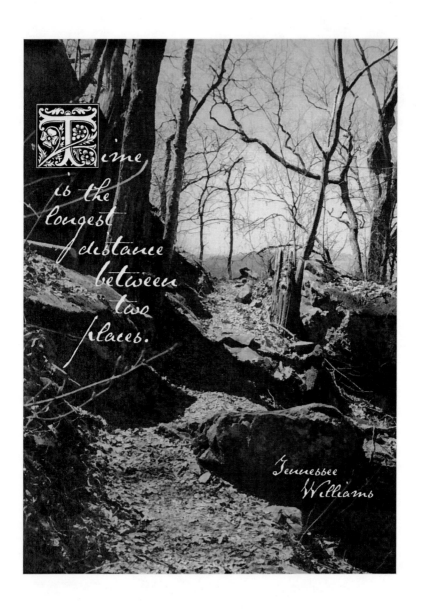

Time is the longest distance between two places.

Tennessee Williams

six | Time Into Space

At a campsite in Virginia with a spectacular view overlooking a valley known as "God's Thumbprint," I met up with a group of section hikers who intended to section-hike the entire Appalachian Trail by taking one week once a year to accomplish the goal. They were no less committed or passionate about the trail as any thru-hiker. When we met, they had started walking north from Georgia seven years before; and there we were at the same exact point that had taken me seven weeks to get to. There is something to be said for both approaches to the long path.

Descent into Spring

Waiting is part of the journey, part of accomplishing the goal. Walking through the barren landscape of the trail in late winter, it is hard to remember what a warm breeze feels like. Yet beneath what appears dead and dry, new life is germinating in the stillness. Sometimes the emergence of that life is sudden.

Several weeks into the hike, I had the astonishing experience of walking from winter into spring, the two seasons distinctly separate yet appearing like parallel strata, literally separated by a discernible line.

Hiking through infinite shades of brown and grey on a steep descent to Davenport Gap, northern gateway to the Smokies, small points and spirals of green pushed up through the mat of dead leaves in increasingly sudden measure. Dark, leafless limbs hung against the sloping ground, soft greys of an almost indiscernible beginning, merging suddenly into living green. Buds and small succulent leaves unfurled in vibrant golden green hues, electric with sunlight shot through the brilliant colors. Spiraling fiddleheads and trees opening into flowers cast color in every direction. It was pure visual sound, a newly awakened song of celebration. This was no gradual crescendo, but an almost violent blast of life and color.

I came to an abrupt stop in the middle of the trail, the penetrating sight catching my breath away. Light and shadow hung against the purple backdrop of the mountains: a living, breathing sanctuary of extravagant proportion. Winter's dull colors were not far above the green, the width between the seasons a mere leap apart. Another hiker approached as I stood in dumbfounded revelry. "I think I am dying of beauty." He cautioned me not to mention it to anyone else. "People are gonna hear of hikers dyin' of beauty out here and won't hike anymore!" Not a bad way to go.

The way of the spirit is often the way of irony. So it is with the long walk. We strap on a physical burden in exchange for the weightlessness of suspended work and home, families and relationships, to forge a distinct identity in the perpetual flow which is the hike. New depths of the soul are plumbed as things of the spirit freely rise to the fore.

Off the trail or on, it is necessary to discern what interruptions are divine, and which ones are obstacles to the flow that moves us along our path. *To everything there is a season, and a time to every purpose under the heaven,*[15] and the trail has its own: a time to hike in company, a time to walk alone; a time to get up before dark and hike as the stars fade into day, a time to hide an extra hour in the sleeping bag. A time to rest.

Just as trees let go of dead leaves before the new can emerge, certain phases in our life must run their course before new growth can occur. To cling to the old only because it is familiar can forfeit what the new season has to offer.

Space Before Time

Most thru-hikers measure the trail not so much in time as in space. When meeting up with a fellow hiker unexpectedly, you generally don't hear "I haven't seen you in weeks!" but instead, "I haven't seen you since West Virginia!" Whatever happens seems to primarily take place in space; time is simply the marker of an event that comes into its fullness. Time withers like fallen leaves along the trail and is swept under the spangled display of living branches held against the sky, tracing a path to memories soon forgotten. As

---

[15] Ecclesiastes 3:1

we walk, we weave a color never before seen in the mysterious tapestry of the warp and weft of time and space.

Time on the thru-hike does not necessarily make an indelible impression as it passes, not unlike the travel-hardened soil of the Appalachian Trail itself, which in many places reveals no evidence of the countless footfalls that have further pressed it into place, yet somehow invisibly underscoring its existence.

Some mysteries are not revealed until the conclusion of a matter, if at all.

Before I left for Georgia, I could not shake the sense that pregnancy was the perfect symbol of the hike: the nexus of space for something to grow in time. While questioning such intuition generally brings one no closer to understanding, if the analogy were to hold, this was certainly not going to be a full-term "pregnancy" assuming the hike was to be completed in six months. However, the impression remained as I began the hike, and I had all but forgotten about it as the months went by until late one summer afternoon.

Several of us had just crossed the Susquehanna from the sleepy town of Duncannon, Pennsylvania, stopping for a brief rest at the first shelter out of town. A couple of southbound section hikers who were also former thru-hikers were setting up for the night. We engaged in typical trail talk: how long we'd hiked, when we hoped to finish, what the next section was like.

When one of the hikers asked me simply how the hike had been, it would have been easy to speak of the countless graces that had been cast along the path up until the present moment; but I found myself instead relating apprehension at not being further along at that particular time of year, wondering what kind of weather we might meet with in northern New England. With an assuring smile, the hiker's exact words to me were "Oh, you don't need to worry; you're still safe in the womb of the middle." As I hadn't shared the pregnancy analogy with anyone, I could hardly believe what I'd just heard a perfect stranger utter. There seemed a divine wink in the words that I was in just the right place at the right time.

The day after arriving home from the trail, I counted up the months and the days from start to finish. An astonishing seven months and three weeks. I was born five weeks prematurely; my mother had carried me in the womb for exactly seven months and three weeks.

No amount of walking according to a schedule could have resulted in such a parallel, what with injuries, or slowed down by weather or visiting friends, or taking a random extra half-day off in the woods or in town. It was an uncanny, unforgettable reminder that new beginnings can take place through the course of a lifetime.

Pacing

Thru-hikers are often asked what it is like to walk the trail for seven months, through fourteen states. Odd as it may seem, I would like to know as well! When I see a map of the east coast, it is hard to grasp my own two feet taking me more than two thousand miles over mountains and hills, through hail and sun, across gaps, over spongy puncheons and through ice-cold fordings, all the while lavishly fueled by a hunger for what I had not yet seen. The experience of thru-hiking was less like accomplishing an event, and more just an awareness of a wildly rambling yet highly focused lifestyle held for seven months' time.

The trail itself could have been one endless loop for all my sense of forward progression. There is little perception of ground gained other than sore muscles and a collection of progressive dates and guidebook listings. Studying profiles of different sections of the trail displaying elevation changes and mileage, I have tried to recollect threading that long path through my awareness all those long hours and miles, but find it nearly impossible to recreate.

I learned to take other hiker's descriptions of forthcoming trail with a grain of salt. A northbounder's typical interface with a southbound hiker, whether a day, section or thru-hiker all pretty much went something like this: "So, how's the final stretch from here to the shelter? I hear the next climb is pretty rough." "Oh, this past section is a breeze! One little hump to get over and then it's a cakewalk all the way to the shelter." What they really mean is a "breeze" along with the quarter-mile of ankle turning rocks, four other ascents and knee-crippling descents before the ten-yard "cakewalk" to the shelter. Or the opposite: "How's the walk to the next gap?" "You'll never make it before dark; much too difficult. Next couple climbs are tough. They'll kick yer butt." Very early on in the hike, words like these were often met with the Eeyoreish messenger's desired result: intimidation.

As the days, weeks and months rolled by, however, these kinds of remarks were fuel for the fire. I grew to relish such comments from the opposition as bonus motivation—and walked on.

Any task cut to size is manageable, even enjoyable. But sometimes a thing is never finished or even started because it does not seem possible to complete.

To attempt the totality of a task without breaking it down into small bits can be to choke action that would otherwise freely flow.

Whether for good or for ill, the opinions of others can have the power to drive our decisions. Ideas are safe enough in the mind, but once borne through word or action they must be reckoned with: and whether strong or unequipped for the rigors of the world, the original idea is shaped by all it encounters. Wise counsel can make the difference between having an idea and placing it into the realm of possibility.

Our mindset is what guides us to the next point in life, illuminated by wisdom, no matter the source. This informs the very next step, which leads to the next and eventually to a whole new outlook. Pacing affords us the time to ask if we are on the path we want. When we rush ahead or push too hard, we can miss cues alerting us to our best route at a crucial juncture. How limited to a moment we are anyway, never possessing more than a single breath or a single step at once.

The trail itself is not strenuous; it is the pace we keep that determines the strain.

Proper pacing, except maybe the kind associated with impatience, can be challenging. Rest is essential—and during the waiting times, it helps to remember that waiting is a form of rest. Yet the monumental effort required by a loved activity easily produces a naturally flowing energy.

On the trail, there are countless chances to see wonders every day that even guidebooks and maps could not explain away: views all the more captivating for the effort required to glimpse them; clean air pouring over pungent earth, the musical accompaniment of a stream; exertion resolved with well-earned meals and deep sleep; a merry tribe of fellow nomads inspired to walk every step between the beginning and the end, however those steps looked.

The way of the spirit is the way of humility, of allowing ourselves to be guided on the course created long before we were there.

Scent of Synchronicity

Hiking out of Vermont, I finally crossed over into the last state that lay between me and the finish. As I neared town, a day hiker approached wearing a t-shirt that read: *How beautiful on the mountains are the feet of those who bring good news!*[16] The previous day, the same verse had come to mind as I pondered the sorry state of my tired feet. Long-distance hikers experience many changes in their feet; constant swelling, blackened toenails, fallen arches, blisters and calluses. When the time comes for the courageous nightly ritual of sock-peeling to reveal what hardly seem be one's own feet, "beauty" is generally not the word which comes to mind. Yet the thought of trail-torn feet, moving with swiftness through rugged terrain bearing a life-giving message, are nothing less than lovely.

I shared the morning's musings with the day hiker, who was ecstatic to meet a thru-hiker. She had been preparing an inspirational talk for a group the following day, and was delighted for an opportunity to share new insights since our meeting regarding the verse and divine synchronicity; the message of hope carried within a person, written on a heart. She wrote my name down and promised to send a care package to Monson, the last accessible trail town in Maine before the northern terminus.

More than a month later in Maine, I approached the trailhead to hitch a ride into town. In less than five minutes, a small pickup stopped; the driver turned out to be none other than the ferryman who took hikers in his canoe across a dangerous section of the well-known Kennebec River. He said I was very fortunate he happened to be driving by at that moment, saying it was typical for hikers to stand and wait at that particular place for an hour or more. Timing.

He dropped me off at the little post office, and sure enough, my New Hampshire friend had sent a box of goodies. I walked the short distance to the nearby hostel reflecting on the kind fruits of such a chance meeting and wearily climbed the stairs to the bunk room.

No sooner had I lowered my pack to the floor when I heard footsteps and an enthusiastic voice calling from the bottom of the stairs: "Mogo? MOGO? Is that you?" It didn't sound like my hiking partners who had been close behind— but who else could it be? The footsteps clattered up the wooden stairs, and suddenly, my friend from New Hampshire and her daughter stepped into the room, our eyes widening in amazement. Passing through town on their way to visit a nearby college, my friend and her daughter had just stopped into the post office to see if I had picked up the package sent weeks before. Stepping forward to give me a hug, she looked momentarily astonished before joyfully

---

[16] Isaiah 52:7

exclaiming: "You smell TERRIBLE! How WONDERFUL!" To her, excessive odiferousness was merely evidence that I had truly been walking the walk. People who are able to see through all the evidence of an effort-filled struggle on the way to becoming more fully ourselves are a rare treasure. *To one, we are the fragrance of death, to the other, the fragrance of life.*

Some people never enter the fullness of an experience because they are afraid of what they might smell, sound, or look like in the process. There is nothing quite as unpleasant on the trail as putting on the daily outfit which has been cumulatively absorbing the effect of hours slabbing through countless gaps and straining up and down ridgeline after ridgeline. There is the moment of repugnance at coming so close to such an unbridled stench, but soon, it is forgotten in the day's challenge forward. The collective scent of a hiker and all the gear that somehow manages to stow away the scent of past hours, days and weeks of accumulated funk is beyond words to describe; it has a presence all its own. Yet, it is an inescapable part of the journey.

When we are in transition or in a place of rapid growth, we can be disgusted at the resulting stench of our own efforts that still have not taken us to the place we long to be. But with time, they will, if we do not give up.

All for the Want of a Gaiter Snap

After pulling off the trail in Vermont to spend a weekend with family and friends in Boston, we had stopped at an outfitter on our way back to the trail for some cold-weather gear. Among the purchases was a pair of long gaiters[17] I had not tried on before buying, as they were the same reliable brand as the shorter ones I'd worn most of the hike.

Arriving back at the trailhead well after dark, we labored under our now heftier packs a short, steep distance to meet up with friends camped within a mile of the road. One of our group expertly strung her tarp among the trees and hospitably invited me to take shelter under its ample roof due to the lateness of the hour.[18]

---

[17] Gaiters help keep hiker's boots and socks free of pebbles, sticks and mud

[18] Not having to take the time to scope out a suitable tent site and unpack the tent and do the reverse in the morning was a considerable timesaver. Staying up late does not generally happen on the trail, and is in fact almost an impossibility after a full day hauling bones, boots and pack for many rugged miles. Hikers are often tucked in for the night not long after the sun goes down; some jokingly refer to 7 or 8 pm as "hiker midnight."

In the middle of the night, a heavy mist became steady rain became a downpour. The otherwise hikerly homelike tarpsite was swiftly transforming into something closer to a poor man's water park. What had been a comfortable indentation in the ground under my sleeping pad was now a shallow bathtub; it was alarming how quickly a little or in this case a lot of water falling from the sky could suddenly have such interrupting force. As the dry area directly in the middle of the tarp was now only adequate for one, I pitched my tent as hastily as my sleepiness would allow, thankful for possessing a leak-proof shelter.

In the morning, I decided to try on the new gaiters for the first time. Ripping open the velcro enclosure and putting them in place, I was dismayed to find one of the snaps necessary for a snug fit completely torn out.

Within a few days we had made it to the next town. I called the outfitter to see about replacing the gaiters, thinking it was probably futile as there wasn't time to send the defective pair back and await new ones: colder weather was coming, miles needed to be made. To my surprise, the store associate cheerfully asked where a new pair of gaiters could be sent overnight; they didn't want the defective ones back. Not having made plans to be anywhere but just a day's hike further down the trail, I opened my guidebook and arbitrarily picked a place that seemed to be a reasonable day's walk away in the next nearby town.

With arrangements made, I hiked on, completely unaware that events were soon to take place that would completely undermine any remaining disbelief I had that a benevolent force beyond our control can precisely order events in ways that never could have been humanly orchestrated.

Clambering down the final descent to the trailhead, I was accompanied by a section hiker interested in joining me on my quest for a hitch into town in order to get some breakfast. We were surprised to emerge from the woods to bumper-to-bumper traffic just beyond the trailhead parking lot. Approaching the nearest car, we learned that the Highland Games were in full swing at the local ski resort, drawing crowds in the thousands to the otherwise small town. The hostel where the new gaiters were being sent was within the resort, so we were about to experience the festivities whether we wanted to or not.

Getting to the entrance of the resort was easy, as buses were shuttling crowds directly from the center of town where our "trailhead angels" had taken us. We were intent on getting back to the trail as quickly as possible, hopeful of making some miles before dark. The hostel was a good distance from the entrance gate, where we stepped into the resort surrounded by hordes of festival goers and walked nearly a mile down a dirt road to get to the door; not exactly a thru-hiker's favorite pastime off-trail. Typically, it is crucial to spend as much time off one's feet as possible before the next day's exertion, and road-walking is particularly exhausting. However, we finally arrived at our destination.

To our surprise and frustration, the hostel manager did not have the gaiters. When pressed, she said a package had arrived, but she had given it to her husband earlier that morning who was working maintenance at the games; his office was a mile away back towards the main entrance to the resort. I didn't bother to ask why "hold for thru-hiker" was not literally interpreted. We had no choice but to head back.

As we plodded back empty-handed in the direction we had just come, mercifully, a resort employee driving past stopped and offered us a ride back to the games.

The employee turned at a fork in the road that led into a part of the resort we had not yet seen. The way led past row after row of tents with Scottish clan name signs clearly displayed in alphabetical order. I remembered one of my favorite professors from college had mentioned something about attending the games; perhaps he was there, or at least someone from his family or others that knew of him. After getting dropped off next to the tents and near the maintenance office with the now highly anticipated gaiters, we first found the tent with the professor's name displayed. A few people sat under the canopy talking and relaxing. I asked if anyone had heard of the professor. "*Heard* of him?" was the laughing reply. "He's here as always, just happens to be taking a nap at the moment. Stick around, he'll be out soon in full regalia."

Making our way to the nearby maintenance office, no one was there but the screen door was unlocked. Hesitating to intrude but emboldened to claim what was mine, I let myself in the door, and there sat my clearly addressed package on a desk.

What turned out to be even more inspiring than the perfectly intact gaiters was a surprise note packed with them that read: *You don't know me but I thru-hiked in '92. You're almost there. Don't be afraid of the Whites and Maine. They are tough, but just pace yourself and you'll do fine. Blessings ><> "Bill and Best Friend" / Bill B., Shipping and Receiving.*"

While pondering the pleasant turn of events and waiting for my professor to awaken, we had time to discover that eating haggis was not going to be necessary ever again, throwing telephone poles looked to be more trouble than fun, and *Amazing Grace* likely sounds better when played by a chorus of bagpipers than any other way.

By the time we returned to the professor's tent, there he was, decked out in traditional garb, looking ready to recite some Robert Burns. We explained what had brought us to the festivities from the relatively austere universe of the trail. Not far into the conversation, we were invited to the family's condo for showers, laundry and lasagna. We quickly decided that we would make up the miles the following day. Enthralled by yet another escalation in the day's delights, as we spun on our heels from the tent to head to the parking lot and our ride that awaited, I almost bumped into a woman and her young son standing close by. I could hardly believe my eyes: it was a good friend from the high school swim team I'd not seen in more than a decade and had regretted losing contact with. The turn of events was unprecedented—amazing grace, indeed.

If the day's synchronicity were not enough, there was more to come.

Several days later, having crossed over the border into Vermont, two of us had missed a poorly marked right-angle turn in the trail and continued along an alternate path that led to edge of another ski area. We had planned to meet up with others for a respite from the cold at a cozy inn just off the trail. With maps to guide us, rather than backtracking to the trail, we walked down a steep ski slope towards what looked from a distance like a conglomeration of neon-colored bubbles. As we drew closer, it was clearly some sort of tent city, but the tents too large, too colorful and placed too close together to be that of backpackers. There were no campers in sight. By the time we arrived at the bottom of the slope, it was almost dusk. We stepped inside the nearby lodge and found that the resort was hosting an outdoor expo. A few vendors were still setting booths up as we prepared to head back out, but not before asking just out of curiosity if the vendor who made my gaiters was going to be at the expo. We found they were indeed there, just not in the building at that moment. We were fortunate to get a ride straight from the lodge by one of the outfitter representatives also planning an evening at the inn.

A good night's rest later, a large group of us sat together at breakfast swapping stories of the previous few days of walking. As I was sharing about the broken gaiter snap and the lengths we'd gone through to replace them, a man seated with some others across the room suddenly stood up, approached our table and extended his hand to me. He introduced himself as a representative of the company we'd been discussing. He apologized for the inconvenience of the broken gaiters and handed me an expedition-quality pair of gloves with the company's logo prominently displayed as a "token of appreciation for continued business," and turned and sat back down with his colleagues.

Had we not missed the turn in the trail, we would never have encountered the expo or encountered the company's spokesman. Had the gaiter snap not been broken, and the replacements not sent to the wrong place, I never would have seen my former professor or old friend from high school.

The *coup de grâce* was just days after returning home from the trail. I was visiting the church I had attended just weeks before leaving for the trailhead in Georgia. As I was sharing with a few people that I had come home from walking the Appalachian Trail, one broke in and said, "You know, there's someone else here that hiked the trail a few years ago, you should meet him!" Within minutes, I was introduced to the veteran thru-hiker—whose name was Bill. Said he'd thru-hiked in 1992. I asked him if by any chance he worked at a certain local outfitter. He did, in shipping and receiving. Without saying a word, I reached into my wallet and pulled his note out. I'd decided to keep the tradition of carrying it with me after it had accompanied me to the very end of the trail. I honestly do not know who was more astounded in that moment. I asked him who "Best Friend" was; not to my great surprise, his reply: "God."

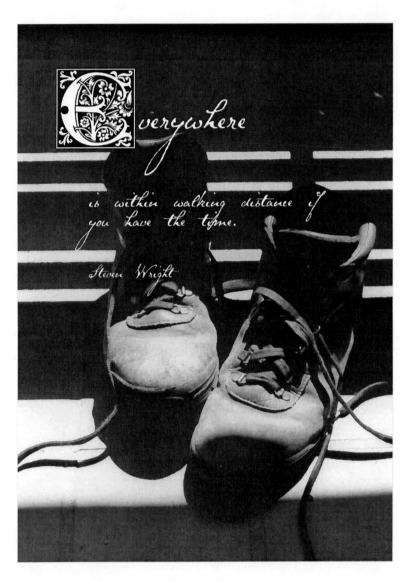

Everywhere is within walking distance if you have the time.

Steven Wright

| *seven* | A Walk Within |

The hike itself may actually be incidental to the monumental spiritual dredging that can take place while walking. Yet, while it is the walk that leads to this soul-searching, one cannot really be defined apart from the other. The trail was both crib and crucible: a place of safety[19] and relative security while at the same time, a perfect environment to expose personal limitations, identify new strengths, and ultimately, a place to be refined.

To step away into the day and have an entirely new view to work out one's thoughts is tremendously cathartic. The lack of intellectual stimuli naturally creates an environment for this nonlinear but nevertheless poignant experience of the spirit, and leaves one more open to pondering the mysteries of existence.

Trail Not to Scale

A thin space that leads the avid walker past innumerable signs of life and growth and decay and regeneration, the trail provides daily reminders in gratitude for little things, like the tiny pair of scissors hidden in the Swiss army knife so handy for cutting Moleskin[20] for a hotspot before it turns into a blister; camaraderie with fellow sojourners most every single night at the shelter or in a ring of tents; the intoxicating scent and murmur of the wind in

---

[19] Despite its remoteness, the Appalachian Trail is statistically safer than the safest small town in the nation.

[20] Heftier than a band-aid, akin to felt with a sticky back, and tremendously handy for covering blisters and potential blisters.

balsam firs. The lilting song of the white-throated sparrow. Soaking one's feet at midday in a cold stream after many long miles.

Yet, for all its relative pleasures, one of the greatest joys of the trail was drawing ever closer to completing it. There was no need to try to conjure up some kind of motivation to finish: the joy of anticipating what was around the next bend in the trail was all-consuming, even as it all pointed to culmination.

When days seemed short and the path ahead too arduous, the reminder of what we were walking directly towards every time we positioned our feet back on the trail in the morning kept things focused, knowing that it was nothing but a matter of steps before arriving at the final destination. No matter how discouraging things might be at any point in time, or even when zeal was unflagging, the remedy was always the same: walking just one more day.

Shifting into a new season, it can be both unnerving and enervating watching what is known and familiar pass aside, making way for the new. All one can really do is watch and wait and act accordingly in the moment. The trail is nothing if not a study in transitions.

Although the massive distance is almost incompatible with sound thinking, having the confidence or even the folly to claim one's intention to trek more than two thousand miles point to point is nevertheless wildly freeing. The hiker knows that even if it is not achievable for one reason or another, it is still going to be fun trying.

Not every mile has a gloriously cascading waterfall or awe-inspiring view into a picturesque valley; sometimes it is just many weary miles of the same dirt path littered with rocks and roots. And while the tree canopy overhead provides welcome shade, other times it feels like a windowless tunnel offering no escape. With all the mountains to climb, there is usually no fanfare for what is no less an achievement for its being unspectacular.

Despite the sometimes excruciating effort, the method is simple and unchanging: placing one foot in front of the other, however unconsciously, but nevertheless firmly, in the desire to continue. Many steps later, it is not only possible to arrive at the goal, it is impossible not to.

Having a goal simplifies the way, and like a trail definitively cutting its way through the trees, certain decisions are naturally made for us to keep to the narrow way. The trail teaches the basics of stepping into new beginnings, of the importance of enjoying getting there—and at times of the peril along the way. Joys and sorrows unexpected, but all worth it for the sustaining purpose.

There is no need to carry fear when you know how your gear works and have what it takes to be fully covered in an unforeseen event. As one trail maintainer wisely observed, what is the use of worrying about what you can't prepare for anyway?

The first time camping at a high elevation and awakening to a violent thunderstorm was terrifying; but at some point, a shift occurred. There was nothing we could do to stop the weather, so it only made sense to instead enjoy the wild display of power that would never be experienced under ordinary circumstances.

With so many unknowns, the one thing we can prepare for as we go is how we will respond when the unexpected comes: our attitude. Knowing we have ceaseless access to divine encouragement no matter where we find ourselves in life makes it easier to step away from becoming confined by fear and choose instead to grow. It is a choice relentlessly given, even if it does not always come in the way we expect.

When the challenges of the trail seem stacked against its benefits, its remoteness is one of the advantages to staying the course. While it is not impossible, it is difficult to leave. Doubts tend to come when struggling alone up a rugged hill when the day should have ended five miles back at the last decent campsite, not when sitting at a table brimming with food and drink and fellowship of the on-foot community.

On the trail, we are captured in living landscapes, making messages and designs with our hands and feet, our breath curling invisible patterns back into the atmosphere, mingling with the silent breath of the living things arching under, over and all around us. The whole body listens to this awareness on the trail, translates to the heart the sheer joy of existence. This wordless whisper is what draws every long-distance hiker back again and again to the trail, and whether in the elements or only the memories, nothing can erase the sense of home. Home is where we can be ourselves.

Identity

At trail's beginning, some hikers do not yet feel qualified to identify themselves as a 'thru-hiker;' it just sounds too strident an assumption so early in the game. Perfect strangers encountered at trailheads or in towns inquiring how long one intends to hike are quick to support such a doubt. Quizzically raised eyebrows that betrayed "Are you *kidding me?*" and all the while smiling patronizingly were common reactions to our assertion that we intended to take the very long walk.

For some, it just takes a little time to come fully into ownership of the thru-hiker title, even if the course is set. Perhaps there is more confidence in responding "I'm headed to Maine" when lighting the camp stove is a less volatile proposition, or the first blisters have callused over, or the stench of one's efforts builds to a pitch only the very brave can bear.

But the decision to walk the trail in its entirety is like any solemn vow. More than just a desire to finish, it is a commitment to occupy every step along the way, regardless of what that decision ultimately involves. To take it for all that it is and all that it is not, and to take it as it comes.

For others, there is absolutely no question as to the felt legitimacy of being a thru-hiker and covering the distance. For most, day after day of walking through creation, camping, making new friends, and the wondrous conditioning of the physical body and the spirit within were more than enough reason to keep going.

Desire creates a flow that carries the thru-hiker past many roots, rocks, slippery logs and other hazards along the way. The path welcomes every step forward, even when rocky and laborious, eventually and without fail rewarding the bone-weary traveler that the struggle is not in vain, that the pain is just part of the birthing of a life lived to the full.

Still, the trail in its remarkably unsophisticated way can perplex even the most well intentioned and best equipped. One cannot walk for months on end without squarely facing one's own humanity in all its glory and pathos, wonder and buffoonery. There are days when the trail and the very weather seemed to have conspired against us as we risked life and limb for a taste of freedom only found among trees which face no roads or buildings, growing from unadorned ground that exists for no other purpose than to stand in silent glory beneath the sky.

Doubts can create stumbling blocks along the way. You may grow weary along the way and question your ability to stay on course. You may even leave the path. Lack of supportive voices along the way, including one's own, may be a primary cause for such a decision.

But the story does not have to end there.

Our identity is not found in the mistakes we have made, or the reputation we have created through our choices. Our identity is who we are created to be. Our blueprint is hidden in our Designer who is also a restoration expert, always striving to bring us back to the place we are intended to be: confident in who we uniquely are. Perhaps there is no other purpose for the excessive clamor of one's thoughts on the long walk than to raise to the surface what needs healing. The soul is on a relentless pursuit of peace, and the trail is an unparalleled sanctuary to seek it.

Despite companionship or solitude, blisters, sunsets, birdcalls and whispers of wind, leaves bending in the rain and mud-soaked socks, the hiker keeps plodding along in boots muddy and dusty, treads wearing thin, worn laces. Looking more like years of wear than mere months.

The path spreads continually before us, never nudging us away, never talking us out of the journey. The thru-hike is slung between raw survival and elevated moments not achieved through lesser means. The elements necessary to maintaining momentum are humble enough: sweating, tripping, swearing, groaning—at times questioning—yet unremittingly committed to the way.

Even when we rationalize why it would be better to leave, something keeps drawing us back. This is the path of grace, and it is full of forgiveness: no matter how many tears or expletives are in the wake behind us or what will pave the way in front of us, the path perpetually remains open, offering no other response to all which has transpired than to simply keep going; that somehow, around some bend, the effort will be revealed as worthwhile.

Walk of Grace

The hunger to see what was around the next bend in the path was never satiated, not even in seven months of walking. The long walk north began with a vivid sense of unrequited freedom long held at bay, and hunger for more of something that was hard to articulate at the time. Much if not most of it was a desire to let go of fruitless attempts to control things that cannot be changed, and to enjoy things that came unbidden.

There are fewer distractions on the trail to cloud the awareness that on any journey of life we are constantly changing, progressing. And while our path is narrowed by what we have or have not chosen, nevertheless, every day presents limitless possibilities to choose anew, wide as the sky overhead. Everyone chooses a trail to run through the center of their lives: every trail is life-changing, and presents multitudes of new choices as one encounters the unseen and unforeseen all along the way.

Particularly in the early days of the trail, but sustained throughout, not really knowing what a given day would hold was marvelously liberating. The confines of self-imposed cynicism passing itself off as the only true wisdom was more a byproduct of not taking the time to see opportunities that existed than actually produced by circumstances. Perhaps there is a link between simplicity and trust: fewer choices make for easier decisions, or at the very least, less complicated variables. On the trail, dedication to staying the course is the foundation of every decision: to simply show up with everything, regardless of what the previous day's events held, and keep walking through whatever weather to accomplish the goal. To trust it is even possible.

Over time, the hiker eases into an adventurer's view of life: ceaselessly new, marked by love of the journey, despite washed out bridges, gloomy afternoons alone or walking fifteen miles on a blister. The ability to keep walking is proof that *mercies are new every morning.*

Three-quarters of a year in the scheme of things is not a long time. Yet it is more than sufficient to redirect the entire course of a life. The trail represents stepping away from a familiar path to one that is far more radical, simply because it is unknown. A deliberate turning from one existence, to step into the new. It has been observed that change happens when the pain of staying the same exceeds the pain of changing. Pain is an indicator that something needs to shift, and when prolonged, something that needs to be healed.

The hike was a parenthesis in time to muse and to dream, but ultimately, it was a gateway to live a life of fuller abandonment to essential callings. It was a conscious return to simplicity in answer to a yearning to live life, even if for a season, according to its most primary elements. A time and a place to refocus, to clearly see what needed to take place next.

Each of us
is merely a small
instrument; all of
us, after accomplishing
our mission, will
disappear.

Mother Teresa

eight | Mortality

Reminders of our temporality generally come when least expected. Walking the trail brings many opportunities to overcome unsubstantiated fears, while at the same time growing in respect for what is larger than we are. Caught in the midst of circumstances and environments capable of our undoing, we are led to the obvious conclusion: we are not the ones ultimately in control.

Batteries, Bulls and Lighting Bolts

Early one morning, just steps into the day's journey, I found myself reflecting on the extent to which fear had characterized my life in the years before leaving for the trail. Fear of stepping out into the unknown and living as an artist, fear of how I might be perceived or judged by those dubious of my making my own way; fear of living motivated by fear. I prayed a short, bold prayer to be released from fear. The day was like most any other along the trail, except for a particularly long traverse over several clear-cut balds.

With high winds and rain clouds darkening the sky, I neared the first exposed summit, almost lost in the heavy condensation. Wind-driven clouds whipped over the edge of a narrow col near the top, a sight like that of clouds streaming over the wing of an aircraft in flight. Wind caught the edge of my pack cover which began to flap frantically like a sail, tethered by a thin cord attached to my pack. With the sudden stillness not unlike that which follows after hypnotically watching the last car of a long freight train pass by, swiftly retreating clouds suddenly lifted where the veil of mist had concealed all but a few yards of the pathway ahead. I found myself closer than I could have imagined to the edge of a precipice and a view deep into the valley below. Fear of falling, of being blown over the edge was followed by a surge of adrenaline, transcended by a strange exhilaration. Had my prayer been answered that quickly? Maybe. The day, however, was not over yet.

Several more miles and I arrived at Overmountain Shelter, an old barn which made for a deluxe resting place. Many hikers were taking an early day to enjoy the novelty of four walls and the luxury of a full upstairs; comparatively palatial accommodations compared with the modest three-sided shelters that typically served as home base. Light filtered in through narrow gaps between wide boards, reminding me of hobos in a boxcar—we weren't that far off the mark. Talk of a coming storm rippled through the otherwise lighthearted conversation. After a short break, I decided to hike on to catch up with some friends who were further on up ahead. Moving out from the shelter and heading back to the trail under the darkening sky, a hiker named Ghost approached, confirming word of the storm.

Not even a quarter mile from the shelter, the rains began. Stepping away from the covering of treeline past scattered shrubs and stony outcroppings, the increasingly barren landscape soon gave way to the first grass-covered hill. The trail rambled over several more balds before any semblance of shelter.

The rain came down harder, literally: chunks of hail began to crazily bounce over the grey-green landscape as if scattered from a giant salt shaker, the view increasingly impressionistic through my rain-studded spectacles. Leaning into the weather, the elements seemed bent on matching my stubbornness with their own. Kicking the raindrops out of the way, they fell with such a speed my damp footwear transformed before my very toes into oddly shaped buckets, with a superb ability to retain water. The sloshing and wheezing sounds unique to splashing about in waterlogged boots created a somewhat pleasing counter rhythm with the syncopated suction of my boot soles against the muddy trail; in the circumstances, a pleasant distraction.

I walked on in spite of the weather, my fears and better sense of judgment; what else was there to do? The shelter was too far back to return, and there were several more balds to traverse. As the elevation rose and one thunderclap followed another, the frailty of existence had never seemed so apparent.

Finally clearing the last of the trees before emerging onto the bald, the rumbling of thunder and closely following flashes of lightning became a more consuming thought than wet feet.

I found myself muttering words something to the effect of: "God, I know you see me here. You know the number of my days, and if this is my last, it is in your hands. I am not going to be afraid." What pillars of electricity could harm me if it wasn't my time? And if one was going to deliver a mortal blow, I couldn't escape anyway—so what is the use of worrying?

I will not lead the reader to believe I took my time hiking through that storm; in fact, I moved with a speed I didn't know I possessed. Yet it was with a lightness of heart, and a new confidence in the Unseen. I could only believe a swift answer to the morning's request for trust to displace fear had come.

As I staggered on against the high winds over the two balds, I began to notice bare oval patches in the grass appearing at random intervals on either side of the path, with no apparent cause for their existence.[21] I plodded on, increasingly content that I had seen the worst of the storm and could now enjoy my newfound peace. However, the day wasn't over—not quite yet.

A few miles more and the trail crossed a road, led back into the woods, and into a deep hollow rimmed with trees silhouetted against the fading dusk. Purplish streaks of lightning streaked laterally across the sky in soundless pulsing pattern, the last of the storm gone by.

The sky cleared a bit and irregular patches of deep blue appeared in the gloaming between intermittently foreboding and peaceful-looking clouds. There was just enough light to see I had just entered pastureland.

I settled into a peaceful stride, happy to be completing the last mile of the day. The trail crossed a high sloping meadow, a huge grassy bowl rimmed with trees, losing color as night fell. As I stepped carefully to avoid the cow "mines," a herd of several dozen cattle with calves gradually became apparent in the dim light. As I neared the part of the pasture where most of the dark shapes were gathered, I heard a loud "maaaugh" that seemed unmistakably directed at me.

As I stepped closer to the herd, I heard the same animal emit a more authoritative and resonant "MAAAUUGH." I paused for a moment, pondering this intense escalation of bovine verbiage. I quickened my pace, finding the mines increasingly difficult to discern in the muddy light. This last foray up the sloping pasture was suddenly framed in what could only be identified as a threatening "moo." I had very little time to ponder this apparent shift in my

---

[21] I did not think of the odd patches in the grass again until I was midway through Virginia listening to another hiker's stories: "Hey, remember those strange, round patches of bare soil all over Jane Bald? Well, veins of iron ore run all through it, shallow enough to attract lightning bolts; the bare patches are places where lighting struck and burned all the grass away."

admittedly limited experience with bovine-to-human communications before I saw in the waning daylight a dark shape moving with studied swiftness in my direction.

It did not take long to evaluate the surroundings and locate a sizable boulder poised reassuringly under a large tree, perhaps a dozen yards behind. As I hastily made my way down the hill, I reached for my headlamp which in keeping with the day, had become little more than a novel storage container for dead batteries. Naturally, the spare set was buried in a small kit somewhere near the bottom of my top-loading pack. Epiphanies regarding things such as packing a pack with wisdom and efficiency know no time or season. Rooting around to find the fresh batteries, it became necessary to unload most of my gear, which soon lay hastily spread about at the foot of the boulder in classic "explosion in an outfitter store" fashion.

By the time my fumbling hands found the batteries, the entire herd of cattle had moved down the hill to the suddenly rather modestly-sized rock. I recalled a story I'd heard in childhood about a woman charged by a buffalo that had climbed the only available tree to escape but could not get one foot out of reach of the buffalo, who proceeded to lick her foot right down to the bone. As I stood in the center of the rock surrounded by these close cousins of the buffalo, I looked up and searched the limbs above somewhat frantically to see if any were low enough to climb into, but high enough to prevent my becoming an unintentional salt lick.

The good news was that the branches were well beyond reach of even the tallest of the cattle; the bad news was they were out of my reach as well. Stretching on tiptoe, I was able to rest my palms against the lowest branch hanging over the rock. I attempted to hoist myself to safety, aware that my best efforts could likely end in more than just my gear scattered under the tree.

I experienced the concept of herd mentality vividly that day: when one cow moved, five or six others would move simultaneously, as if one single animal. Truly one of the most peculiar sights I have ever witnessed. Every few seconds, one then several would move in this odd, synchronized fashion ever closer to the rock. It was a fascinating display of some kind of collective unconsciousness at work, to a yet-as-unknown end.

I still hadn't located the batteries, and it was almost completely dark. A few spindly legged calves lingered near their mothers. I concluded that the entire posse of cattle was conspiring to obliterate the pathetic interloper who could only mean trouble, possessing such a loathsome odor. For all intents and purposes, it did not seem I should have been there. But there I was; there was no going back or getting around it. Finally: batteries found. But before I could fully load the flashlight, the amorphous cluster of hides and hooves had reached the perimeter of the rock. Throughout the quarter hour duration of my stand, I'd attempted to reason with the cows that I was nothing more than a humble guest of their lovely pasture on my way to Maine via Tennessee, if they could be so kind as to let me pass. Their only response was to press closer to the rock. Intellectual superiority seemed my only remaining alibi, and this was increasingly in question. I raised my voice, speaking in a variety of authoritative tones, hoping to persuade them of my cause. The herd pressed in closer, every glassy eye fixed on me, unwavering. I was still outnumbered.

I began to wonder what it would be like to spend an entire night having a staring contest with a couple dozen potentially omnivorous cows. Maybe my assumption that I was the brainy superior was bunk; perhaps this was a particularly enlightened group of bovine activists who felt it was high time to balance the score between the consumption habits of cows and humans. This issue was resolved sooner than I expected, with no obvious winner of the stare-down. Fear had reached the ceiling where it could go no further, becoming stale, boring, useless. One of the cows, bolder than the others and closer to the rock, suddenly lowered its head and began to nudge my sagging pack leaning against the rock, apparently enticed by the salt-saturated hip-belt. The remains of barely warmed-over fear blossomed into swift indignation that my backpack would be marred. Pack innards were still strewn about haphazardly, which I began to enthusiastically restuff, all the while verbally chastising the wide-eyed, unblinking cows for so cavalierly tampering with my possessions.

Swinging my pack in place, suddenly more curious than apprehensive about the likelihood of being stalked, I strode up the pasture past the stand of waiting cows, the dumbfounded lot still in a crescent around the lone rock and tree.

Finally reaching my friends camped a short distance beyond the pasture, I shared my story, laughing at what now seemed silly, unfounded fears until someone spoke up: "You know, there actually were bulls in that pasture."

Too Late to Call Home

Just south of Warren, New Hampshire stood a condemned house steps from the trail, formerly owned and occupied by the Park Service. Commandeered by the thru-hiking community and dubbed the "Atwell Hilton," the rickety building had been adopted by a volunteer caretaker named Dizzy B, who kept the outdoor fire ring well stocked with wood and a generous supply of beer for endlessly thirsty hikers.

There were perhaps three of us the night I stayed there, and as we sat around the fire, Dizzy B had sobering words to share. "This is where I tell all the hikers not to call home if you want to finish the trail. Chances are, if you find out that something is wrong, by the time you go and come back, it will be too late to finish."

I could not have anticipated the news I received upon reaching the town of Warren and calling home the next day. My remarkably healthy and active grandfather had begun rapidly losing weight, and after much pressure from the family finally paid a visit to the doctor, only to find out it was pancreatic cancer. He had just weeks to live.

My parents had planned to visit me in the next few days, and with the news, we changed course and drove twenty four hours to and from my grandfather's place for the immensely bittersweet chance to be together one last time.

Two journeys were drawing to a close, bonding us inexplicably, taking all distance between us away as we moved to the finish lines laid before us.

Goose Eye

There is a wild glory in wilderness that seems to settle even between the twigs on the ground and what can seem at times to be a graceless and bitter wind blowing one's comfort off course. Being confronted with one's mortality is usually in tandem with an unforgettable experience. Despite assuredly many opportunities, I hadn't really tasted it until nearly 1,900 miles of walking were behind me.

Toward the end of a bitterly cold day in early fall moving through particularly rugged terrain, I stepped out from the relative protection of treeline onto a broad granite dome to feel my entire body and closely following pack hooked and encircled by the strongest gust of wind I'd ever experienced. I was approaching the descent of Goose Eye Mountain in Maine, a granite escarpment with steeply sloping walls. The trail curved over its barren, severely curved surface towards a border of scraggly alpine trees.

Under the best of circumstances, negotiating the pitch and smoothness of the dome would have been a challenge. When I emerged from protective tree line out onto the exposed dome, a fierce wind took hold. The need to quickly befriend gravity before meeting under less voluntary circumstances became imminently clear. As I lifted my foot to take the next step, lateral lines of wind like an invisible net tugged me to the ground. Colliding with forces stronger than my ability to choose my way on my terms was underscored by the necessity of dropping to my knees to be as inconsequential to the wind as possible.

Paralyzed by the knowledge that I could not proceed without being toppled, I hugged my knees and waited for the fierce blast to dissipate. A small eternity seemed to pass as I waited, somewhat morbidly curious what would happen if it didn't let up. The awareness that the mountain was utterly indifferent to my predicament pervaded my consciousness as thoroughly as earth reclaiming a body—and I didn't rule out that this might be the day the process was going to start.

Water once flowing in rivulets over the domed rock surface had frozen into wide patches of black ice where the blazes led. There was nothing to hold on to, only the hope that I would somehow be able to navigate across the surface of the rock without major incident. At the base of the pitch, tree limbs weathered silver looked like broken bones knit in a sharp jumble. Under any conditions, negotiating the acute angle would have been a challenge, not unlike maneuvering down the broad side of a giant egg. As I attempted the next step, a fierce gust tugged at me as if I were being laid claim to by invisible cords.

Never had I felt so finite, so capable of suddenly extinguishing at the slightest waft. I harbored no suspicion of divine malevolence at work in the indifferent circumstances, just a direct acknowledgement of a power unfathomably beyond my own. As I clung to the rock pondering what condition I might be in by the time I could finally resume my way, I felt for the first time on the hike and perhaps my life the absolute and insoluble impartiality of nature—what business had I to pass through such savage and holy places? I asked silently, desperately to be able to move off the mountain, realizing as never before the power of Sovereignty. If it were the Creator's will to see me swept into oblivion, nothing I could possibly do would alter that course. Like sinew exposed, the hide was stripped away to reveal the inner workings of my essential being: mortal. I was thankful my mother could not see me.

As shadows were lengthening, I was sure my newly adopted hiking companions backpacking for the week from Germany would already be settling in at the nearby shelter, presumably wondering what had become of the crazy American. Taking off my pack and letting myself roll down the dome until the pines at tree line could catch me up in their gnarled limbs seemed the only recourse should the wind not let up. But even as I blandly considered the colorful assortment of possible effects: splintered bones, jagged scratches, purpling bruises and pitch in my hair, the gust began to lessen. I slowly straightened and gingerly picked my way over the swaths of ice on the slanting, bare surface, feeling caught in some wilderness version of an M.C. Escher.

A phenomenon not unlike seeing one's life pass before the mind's eye takes place in such moments; a colliding of past dialogue and petition, idle comments and questions, the sum total of all thought and inquiry however indirectly or directly toward the Almighty. All at once this collection seemed dull, paltry and almost flippant set against such severe splendor, unleashed as effortlessly as a breath; and I, with such a limited objective: to transport my limited flesh out of the pathway of forces so radically capable of my undoing. Prayers at such times were usually one word in length: "God!" or "Help!" or something far less repeatable but just as honest—prayer nonetheless.

Carrabassett

Waking to a cold drizzle tenting in a sheltered col between Saddleback and Saddleback Junior in Maine's Mahoosic Range, the rain continued steadily as four of us packed up soggy tents and settled into our mutual paces for the day. We decided to meet up at the next shelter for a break and scheme how far to go and where to camp that night given the foul weather. Though seasoned thru-hikers at that point who had seen just about the worst that the trail could dish out, the strain nevertheless had taken its toll. Protecting what strength remained to get to the end was essential.

A few miles north later, we arrived at one of Maine's infamous "baseball bat" shelters. The floors of these so-named shelters were comprised of small logs that ran from front to back that roughly had the circumference of baseball bats. As the wind crackled in the brittle branches above, we debated our options between bites of energy bars. Just as we were about to swing our packs in place, someone spoke up with a new idea. "Hey! Why don't we just get in our sleeping bags and wait out the rain by reading and eating? Maybe the rain will stop tomorrow."

Our backpacks were heavy just a day out of town; there was a certain logic in spending time eating some of the weight away. A chorus of groans, exclamations of defeat and playful railing at our deserter arose; our resolve was almost fragile enough to give in to such luxurious temptation. But in less than two weeks we would arrive at the goal of more than half a year's effort and previous year's planning, the end to which every blistered mile, every bite of food and beam of every headlamp ultimately pointed to: Mt. Katahdin. And yet, at some mundane level the day still felt like any other, lost somewhere between the beginning and the end. What really was the rush?

For much of the hike I had enjoyed taking nap breaks in the sun, contemplating the wildlands at overlooks, soaking tired in cool streams. But for some reason, this particular day I had no desire to break the flow of seven months of momentum. Even the prospect of dubious intellectual entertainment by means of the now-bedraggled science fiction comedy paperback that had passed from hiker to hiker the past several hundred miles and now in my possession was not enough to keep me from moving on.

I shouldered my pack and announced I was moving on. My hiking partners could not conceive of the logic of walking out from under the shelter roof in a freezing downpour hardly a day out of town with a heavy pack load, but I was compelled to go. Meeting up with these friends just a few days prior had been tremendously solidifying after many days alone in the cold and uncertainty of what late-season weather would be encountered so far north, near trail's end. Yet, the prospect of recovered solitude for one day felt like a gift; nothing to interrupt the silent song of leaves and branches, just the meditative symmetry of forward motion, one day closer to the goal.

The trail through southern Maine had definitely lived up to its rugged reputation, but for the first time since stepping across the border, level terrain opened up, a respite after many steep climbs and descents. My pace became meditative, almost unconscious.

There is deep silence in the forest not penetrated for days by traveler's voice or footfall. Shapes of lichen and quartz-veined rock shone dully in what was present of late afternoon light. Fragrant, hardy firs combed the dense, deliberate wind into the sound of the sea.

Hours later, the slant of the lean-to roof finally appearing through the trees after the long day's walk in the chilling rain was a relief, even if a fine mist made the roof and walls almost superfluous. Hot soup and tea were welcome company as night fell. For entertainment, I watched my dripping tent hung to "dry" from the previous night of rain billow ponderously in the permeating moisture. Lying as close as possible to the back wall of the shelter, having chinked the cracks between rough-hewn logs with gear to buffer the damp draft, I imagined the likelihood of awakening to mushrooms proliferating on the outer shell of my sleeping bag, and drifted off in fitful slumber.

Awakening the next morning to the third continuous day of rain and packing up, I recalled reading of a warming hut[22] on the peak of nearby Sugarloaf Mountain. As a good day's walk now lay between me and the baseball bat shelter with friends, paperbacks, snacks and a roof overhead, spending a few hours at the hut was one way to close the distance, dry gear and get out of the wet for a while. Seemed like a good plan at the time. Although my final section of guidebook had been clearly marked for my arrival, unbeknownst to me, the post office in the last town had prematurely returned it to my home address, and with it, word that the hut was already closed for the season.

Stepping out into the day, acre after acre of sodden black limbs and jagged foliage pierced the dripping air as if never touched by light. I walked on heartened by the thought of soon being under a warm, dry roof.

When I finally arrived at the half-mile-long side trail leading to the summit in the steadily falling rain, the rocky ascent had become a gushing stream. Were it not been for the sign marking it as a trail, it would have been indiscernible from a small waterfall. I decided it was worth getting a little wetter for the promise of a snug, enclosed shelter just a short climb away. Picking my way among the small boulders, I was amused at my own attempts to preserve my waterlogged boots from further wet. Near the top, after a soaking, sopping climb, the rain seemed to fall clumsily, fell as snow. The stream flowed slowly, slower into deep slush. As the distance to the peak shortened, rocks in the streambed glittered with frost. By the time I arrived at the top, snow was falling steadily.

As clearly as the descent into spring, this was an ascent from autumn into winter. My confidence was fraying badly as I neared the blustery summit. Stepping out of the relative shelter of the trees to the clear-cut area beyond the tight stand of firs, I peered fruitlessly into the vague grey light for next paces. Snow fell like silence, tracing outlines around the trees, rocks, and

[22] Ski areas generally keep huts available for ski staff, and often are left open as a courtesy for thru-hikers in the off-season.

around me. I stepped tentatively away from the trail along what was soon revealed as a gravel road under the heavy curtain of weather. Glancing back, I was alarmed to see that the mouth of the trail had been completely swallowed by the fringe of trees bordering the ski lift area.

The narrowness of the trail in many places is no wider than the natural spaces between the trees: only the blazes painted at intervals on tree trunks and on rocks in the worn path itself announce its existence. Not exactly helpful in blizzard conditions when the trail like the rest of the forest floor is covered in snow, and even the blazes concealed under shimmering white.

The inability to identify any discernible exit produced a sudden sense of claustrophobia: no one knew I was now many paces off the trail. Whirling bits of snow glanced off my now glowingly red legs; I hadn't intended on a rendezvous with a blizzard. What was perfect covering at a lower elevation was woefully inadequate at such an elevation; it was as if I had inadvertently stepped into an alternate universe, frozen in time. I could only hope my footprints pressed into the newly fallen snow would still be detectable enough to lead me back. Competing with the desire to escape the moment for milder elevations was the stronger sense that had I expended this much to find the warming hut, and did not want to waste the effort. For a thru-hiker to commit to an entire mile off trail is no small investment; it didn't seem logical to turn back until finishing the intended course.

Wondering what direction to head next, my eye fell on faint tire tracks and large footprints along an ice-encrusted gravel road lost in the grey, presumably leading to the hut. My own footprints, bleeding mud into the frozen white ground would be my blazes back to the path. The increasingly faint footprints in the snowy gravel traced the way past various hunkering structures and to the edge of visibility. Following in some combination of hope, stubbornness and blind faith, I stepped into the footprints leading somewhere into the grey. Not far down the icy road, I arrived at the hut. Built into the side of the mountain, the entrance was reached by a shallow deck built out on narrow stilts. Stepping out on the well-weathered walkway, the boards were slick with ice. As I inched along to get to the door, I had a sinking suspicion that I would not be drying my gear just yet. Climbing over the handrail enclosing the entranceway, I gripped the doorknob—locked tight. Not pickable. I tried not to think of how long it would be before help came if I slipped on the ice and fell under the deck. Easing back over the railing, I once more made my way along the treacherous walkway to firmer ground. Following the double set of footprints back the way I had come, with tremendous relief, I found the elusive gap in the trees leading back to the side path.

Climbing back down the small waterfall to the home territory of the trail, the descent to the valley began.

As the path wound its way out of the forest and flanked the mountain, the narrow ledge of the pathway seemed held in place by a thick fog banked up against the rugged contours of the mountainside. A faint murmur quietly increasing in volume from somewhere beneath the cloud line began to rise, sounding at first like traffic in the distance; perhaps a ghost highway, as the closest road of any kind was well out of earshot. With each step, the noise intensified until the hissing, sloshing sound of rushing water was unmistakable. The grey ribbon of the river finally appeared, tumbling furiously past trees, past me, too busy to become acquainted—except on its own terms.

Another crucial bit of information I lacked in the guidebook section's absence was the description of the Carrabasett River as "dangerous to cross in high water." It was another quarter mile or so of walking parallel to the turbulent water with no deviation in direction before I began to suspect that the trail was going to cross the river. Within minutes of this inkling, the trail curved directly towards the water, until the path of leaves, rocks and soil disappeared at the water's edge. Looking out across the tumultuous flow, my fears were confirmed by the white blaze on a tree at the opposite bank.

A narrow double-plank footbridge extending a short distance across the water was anchored near the shore, bobbing with the torrent at its opposite end. No safe passage presented itself. The choice was simple: upstream or downstream to find a place to cross. Casting my gaze as far downstream as possible, the river began to bend southwards, and within a short distance was out of sight between the barren trees. There did not appear to be a way across, and then, I saw it: a grouping of boulders upstream appeared to span the distance, a potential rock-hop to safety.

Stepping off the trail to make my way to the crossing, the bank gradually steepened. I slowly worked my way south, paralleling the river. Newly fallen leaves created the illusion of a smooth carpet to step upon until gravity reminded me that this was well off the beaten path. After laboriously slow passage stumbling into little indiscernible hollows, tripping over rotting concealed logs, and kicking rocks, I arrived at the river boulders—and with sinking, shrinking hope, saw the unspannable gaps between.

Looking even further upstream, another cluster of boulders appeared to be passable. The bank continued its vertical rise, giving little option but to bushwhack a few feet above, rather than beside the water. The most level part of the sloping land above the bank began to edge away from the river, providing only meager footing just at water's edge. A few steps more and the narrow strip of sand finally tapered off into a sheer vertical bank. The only passage now presenting itself was a thin tree bowed over a boulder against the bank, half in the eddying water. As I swung from the tree trunk, my heart beat out a prayerful rhythm, toes pointed and reaching for the rock, hopeful the wet surface would receive the treads of my boots. I began to question my presence of mind as I strained through the drenching rainfall to see any place to cross the increasingly unapproachable river. It seemed every possible hindrance was being placed in the path to see if I would stand the test.

For two hours I continued to bushwhack along the gorged flow. I finally decided to talk out loud, remembering that slurred words and lack of proper judgment signified the onset of hypothermia. Perhaps if I could still follow my own thought process, I could monitor my awareness before it was too late. I wondered if the idea it was even possible to self-test presence of mind was a sign it was already slipping.

I do not know how many times I was utterly convinced I had finally spotted the right configuration of boulders to make it across the river, only to be thwarted. With each false prospective, a piece of hope fell away. My hypothermia-testing small talk now gave way to verbalized prayers: "God! Send your angels to help me!" Fierce resolve to find a way across the river was slowly draining away for blind stubbornness, strangely coexisting with total physical despair. Not even the slightest semblance to safe passage was making itself known. How could I possibly go any farther? What was the point? Going back was not an option; going forward did not seem to be an option; not finishing was not an option. I felt tautly drawn between the utter incapability of crossing and a belief in the Creator's ability to help me find a way.

Reluctantly but resolvedly, I came to the conclusion that the only way across was to get into the water, of course, contingent upon finding a safe place to ford. But how was that even possible? For the second time that day, I gave up completely: not for lack of wanting or even trying, but even the bravest assessment of the situation had not resulted in a way out. And yet, the puzzle remained. I couldn't just walk away from the situation; in fact, I was going to need to walk more deeply into it than perhaps I had ever walked into anything before.

Trying to find boulders to step across above the river had at least made some kind of sense; but now, looking for the least daunting place to get into the water seemed a much riskier pursuit. Realizing that this was not going to be a footbath at the spa, I finally spotted a place that looked shallow enough to step in. As I placed one tentative foot into the river followed by the other, icy water poured into my boots. I tried to cheer myself that at least I was now headed across. The surge didn't even seem that bad after all; maybe it wasn't going to be as difficult as expected.

One step more, the full force of the current nearly pushed me over. Staggering to right myself, I was never more thankful for having a walking stick in each hand. From what could be seen looking through the blur of the racing flow, the riverbed was full of melon-sized rocks. Leaning against the current to avoid getting pushed over, I moved with halting steps away from the bank into deeper water, knowing that a moment of hesitation could result in a lost foothold, or worse, foot entrapment. The distorted surface of the water only revealed a fragmented view of the riverbed and required a painstaking choice for each step. The thought of slipping and getting pinned under the current was terrifying, but as I ventured forth, the fear of lowering my core temperature below a natural ability to raise it became significantly greater.

I continued talking aloud through the ordeal as if I were my own small child in need of consoling. As fear of hypothermia reached a desperate pitch, I suddenly heard myself say in a decidedly authoritative tone: "You will be warm tonight." This was no fruit of my feelings, but rather, a sudden brilliant awareness that as I moved in shaking, terrified, dripping-wet humanity, I had somehow become a mouthpiece of Someone else, who knew no fear. No time to contemplate this. Moments later, I found myself confronted by white water foaming and thrashing against a boulder jutting just above the boiling surface, my course now entirely blocked. Looking over my shoulder, there was no going back; I was almost halfway across. How could I possibly get past this? The hopelessness I had felt at the shore washed over me again. I couldn't see my feet to place the next step. But as I looked into the churning water feeling the greatest terror yet, the following words swept in almost lilting tones from my mouth: "The water is not angry, it is joyful! It is dancing, it is making music with the rock!" Though I still could not see where to step, I nevertheless moved forward, feeling for the first time there was nothing to lose. My dismay swept away with the river's swiftness as I approached the final stretch to the bank; I was almost home free.

But as I moved closer to the edge of the ordeal, I looked ahead and tasted an emotion somehow beyond hopelessness. For the last dozen feet of the river's expanse, the water coursed black and silent, beveling against the bank with a swiftness unchecked by boulders or any visible rocks on the bottom of the riverbed. There was nowhere to step, only an indiscernible depth reflecting back a complete absence of light.

Never had the concept of 'leap of faith' been so graphically or chillingly transmitted to my consciousness. The only course of action was to fling myself toward the bank and hope for the best. As I lunged, I felt all stability leave me, toes dangling some undisclosed distance from bottom. With the water now up to my shoulders, the current swept me along for a few yards before I somehow managed to reach the bank, the thick stand of saplings guarding river's edge snapping, bending as I emerged from the water back into the rainfall, cold and shaken. Finding a faint path through the trees running parallel to the river, I broke into a slow run, my feet clumsy with numbness, a sense of relief surging through my being.

Having bushwhacked for two hours south, I now had some distance to travel to get back to the trail. That the river clearly marked the direction remained my only comfort as it was now critical to get out of the rain as rapidly as possible.

Finally arriving back at the familiar white-blazed footpath angling its way through the woods, I found myself in another quandary: as far as I could see in any direction, countless pools of water lay like broken mirrors scattered amongst the dark, sodden leaves. I was completely soaked through, and even though walking, was beginning to tremble. It was still raining. Where could I possibly pitch my tent in a swamped river valley?

By the time I spotted a sliver of land barely wide and long enough to accommodate my tent, I was shaking intensely and uncontrollably.

Small details can take on unquantifiable significance when a life is precariously perched at the point of no return. Two random purchases, one made in the last town stop likely made all the difference that hazardous day.

Most hikers line their backpack with a plastic bag for added protection from rain and damp. I had recently replaced mine with a heavy-duty trash compactor bag which had so far had proved impervious to countless gear loadings; it was completely free of holes, unlike the one it replaced that increasingly resembled an enormous plastic piece of Swiss cheese. Hikers also commonly keep a cigarette lighter for fire starting. I had carried the same lighter in the front pocket of my jacket all the way from Georgia and used it every day to ignite my stove. For some reason, I had decided just a few days before that it might be useful to have a back-up, and purchased one two days before the river crossing.

As I now lay in my dry sleeping bag bundled in every bit of dry clothing I was carrying, thanks to the trusty trash compactor bag liner, my thoughts turned to the next concern: would my stove light in the rain? I was still shaking incessantly. Reaching for my soaked rain jacket at my feet, I momentarily forgot its hidden contents had joined me in the impromptu river bath. Pulling the dripping lighter out of its pocket, I was not surprised when it didn't light, but now extremely concerned—but wait!—a solution was at hand. Safely stashed in the driest part of my pack was the new lighter. Now, if only the raindrops would oblige my efforts to the end of a little hot cocoa and dinner.

Laying on my side, I unzipped the tent door just wide enough to put my arm out in the steady drizzle. I could only hope and pray the tiny stove pressed as firmly as possible into the spongy carpet of sopping leaves, placed as close to the tent as practicable would actually work. To my great delight and tremendous relief, the stove fired up with the inaugural lighter flick. A few small spits of steam from the burner, and the pan of icy water was on its way to becoming a welcoming bowl of hot soup.

In the middle of the night I suddenly awoke: my excessive swaddling was trapping so much heat I had to remove a layer. I remembered the words spoken in the middle of the river: "You will be warm tonight."

The next morning, the ground was as flooded as the day before but the rain had stopped. As I broke camp, I remembered a dream I'd had the night *before* the river crossing when in the shelter alone.

In the dream, I was in a skiff in the middle of the ocean. There was no land in sight. I was not alone; in the boat with me was a fisherman who knew everything there was to know about fishing. Not knowing much about fishing, I wasn't quite sure what I was doing in a tiny boat with such an expert so far out at sea. Nevertheless, my companion didn't seem to question my presence there. All I remember about him besides what he knew is that his face emanated such a strong light I could not see any of his facial features.

Suddenly, the fisherman pointed to a small heap of water not far over the side of the boat. The heap could not have been more than a few feet in height, but running left to right were a few timbers resembling railroad ties arranged as stairs. The bottom-most step had fallen down on one side, making it unusable. As the angler pointed, he simply said: "Fix that." The words were uttered with authority but not without the understanding that it was a tall order, requiring me to get out of the boat and walk out onto the water.

Looking back up into his face, I told him I couldn't do it. "Yes, you can." His tone was firm, convincing and kind. I realized the only reason I would be able to do it was because he said I could. It was as if he held an account in my name, stocked with full confidence to do things that I would otherwise deem myself incapable of doing.

The next moment, I found myself standing on a rock in the middle of the ocean, the boat and the fisherman nowhere in sight. There was only room enough for one person to stand on the rock, just one in the middle of a long line of rocks reaching as far as I could see to left and to the right, disappearing on either side into an infinite fog.

There are no words to describe the terror I felt knowing I had to step to the next rock as space between each boulder was far beyond what I could span. But neither could I remain standing in place. Moving off the momentary safety of the one rock I stood upon, it seemed inevitable that I would fall in the unspannable gap between and drown. Yet, there was nothing to do but step to the next rock, and I did so in utter hopelessness.

The exact moment I gathered up my courage and lifted my foot, I was suddenly aware of the fisherman standing on the rock with me. As I stepped into what seemed like certain oblivion, one of his arms held me close in a dancers' embrace; and with the other arm extended, our hands clasped, we tangoed to the next rock.

To this day, recalling the dream still evokes the feeling of that foreboding Carrabassett crossing. *When you pass through the waters, they will not overwhelm you.*[23]

---

[23] Isaiah 43:2

We all feel the riddle of the earth without anyone to point it out. The mystery of life is the plainest part of it.

G. K. Chesterton

nine | Earthen Intangibles

There is a certain kind of hush in the woods, a silence kept like a secret in the aching, beautiful gloom on a cloudy day, walking deeper into mist and quiet. Ghostly trees present themselves like shapes painted on silk, appearing for a moment before fading back again into the grey.

The trail was fertile ground for casting a million seeds of thought, letting the wildest dreams and inquiries of the soul run rampant. There was nothing to confront these moments but trees, plants, animals and insects, receiving us unquestioningly as we passed by in the hiddeness. One might suppose there is nothing more peaceful than moving mile after mile through the cloister of the forest without so much as a distraction save the occasional squeak of a scampering chipmunk informing you his territory has been invaded, or the mysterious spiraling song of a veery, or a breath of wind in the leaves.

Yet, silence in the forest is relative. Walking past a splashing stream, its music pushes away another wall into a deeper dimension, speaking volumes without words. The woods are only as peaceful as we are, and often stand in stark contrast to the tangle of thoughts that find their way onto the blank pages of the hours.

When the grade of the trail was smooth and gradual, thoughts were usually light and flowed easily; steep climbs and rougher stretches on the other hand often smoked out great frustrations. Teetering on sharply pointed rocks and slick roots in the path was a reminder even small impediments not only inhibit forward movement but can potentially cause catastrophe. When the heart was heavy, sharp and slippery rocks seemed almost spiteful.

Memories, plans, excerpts from conversations past, well-rehearsed monologues boldly expressed in the safe recesses of the mind; these broken-record phrases—sometimes tormenting, sometimes insipidly dull sometimes provoked a desire to remove the brain and heave it over the closest cliff.

The weight of this almost incessant internal dialogue at times felt far heavier than any physical burden strapped to the back.

With a generous distance to cover in a limited amount of time, taking in all the sights and sounds of the day while walking to the next campsite is a full day's activity and sometimes more. Much energy is expended in the task of simply getting to the next destination. This is not to say there are no blissful moments of dreamy repose or the reverie of reaching the top of a desolate peak with soaring views, but even breaks in town are more about the business of restocking and refueling than relaxing; the hike can be busier than one might imagine.

Seven months spent walking in the woods allows a lot of time to think. Sometimes, too much time to think. Time to pray and yell, sing, shout and dream. Stony ledges high above valley floors at times became impromptu lecterns for bellowing out monosyllabic soliloquies, the distilled accumulation of years' worth of joys unshared, unarticulated sorrows, and vastly trivial frustrations.

There were other times when the rhythm of one's stride seemed to soothe the mind into forgetting that there was ever a time spent not walking in the woods; an awareness perhaps as good as silence. Being lost in this almost dreamlike sense of being such a part of the woods, part of the motion, it is possible to lose a sense of one's presence in the visual fugue of life and decay.

How to Break a Trail

At times, forest fires require closing certain sections of the trail. Torrential downpours, flooding streams and rivers can compromise the footing of the path and require alternate routes. Despite such devastation, the trail is still there. By far, the best way to destroy a trail: neglect it. Within an alarmingly short period, a trail can simply disappear.

When we do not grow or become stalled in life, for whatever reason, we can slowly forget who we are and what our purpose and higher calling are—like weeds overtaking the ruins of a once-beautiful dwelling, obscured by neglect. As we reawaken, we stumble across the ruins and find again what we once knew and loved—and discover it all over again, as if for the first time. Rebuilding takes time, but as with all labors of love, it is time worthily spent.

Creator's Face

It is hard to say what calls us to wilderness, but it is compelling for those who find themselves irresistibly drawn there. The exchange of everyday comforts and securities to satisfy a greater hunger for beauty and soul fulfillment becomes an entranceway into a deeper awareness experienced in few other environments.

Set apart from ordinary constraints of time and decorum and the predictable, the long hike gives the chance to see that reality is only a matter of perception, and that many things can cloud our vision. The walk requires a stripping away of much matter and a delivering of the self into the most basic elements necessary to sustain life in order to see this truth. The way of the spirit is always unpredictable and the thru-hike is a perfect reflection of this mystery. We do our best to prepare for what it might involve, but ultimately, we are at the mercy of what we do not know and cannot project, much less qualify.

Words fail to describe so many elements of the walk. There were times the view looking east or west through the trees produced the same sensation as standing near the ocean. Perhaps some vestige of geologic history could be heard, seen, felt on some subtle yet all-pervasive level. There is an overwhelming sense of an invisible, eternal imprint that moves like an ancient wind through the ephemeral trees, speaking of what once was in years long gone. There were other times when the veil between the unknown and *being* known seemed very thin.

One particularly warm fall day in Maine, I found myself meditating upon the vibrant ground cover of fallen leaves, laid in residual layers of time and decay; small records each of the passage of time, a spiraling descent to earth from a season spent above, arranged in patterns at once random and precise. Every last curling piece of bark so softly, so perfectly laid on small mounds of moss or damp stone pressed into the mud was exquisite to see.

I mused upon the panorama as the work of a consummately accomplished Artist, down to the last quiet cell. It was not a new thought, but this time, something felt different. As I pondered a Creator with power sufficient to call everything into existence from that which was not, my pace began to slow with the weight of the realization of such a One having an even more acute awareness of my existence than I of my own. The tables were turned: I was not the only perceiver; in fact, I was the perceived. I came to a complete standstill in the middle of the trail with the sudden astonishing sense of the Creator's face next to me, great eyes which missed not a thing intently on me as I stood speechlessly, the thoughts which had led up to the vision dwindling into pure awe. I remained rooted in silence for several minutes, awash in an overwhelming sense that nobility was near.

As I thought of the artists and philosophers, scientists and sages I loved and respected most, I had to reconcile my worship with this Being I had caught only the slightest glimpse of: somehow the force behind and beyond every appointment of mind, heart and soul with the most profound discoveries of existence. One so exquisitely, unfathomably sophisticated so as to not need to be seen—yet felt on a level somehow deeper than the most acute of senses.

Wealth Redefined

Some people are intrigued by the idea of a thru-hike but don't have six months to go on a hike. The average thru-hiker doesn't either. For most, the decision to thru-hike is not without a suspended livelihood and loved ones left behind to venture out on a sojourn not everyone supports, much less comprehends. And yet, for many, it is a launching point for embracing an entirely new outlook. The trail experience is about opening the windows and doors and letting the sunlight and wind make its way in: to step away from an insular lifestyle and learn what it is to truly live again.

The thru-hike is less about having the time or resources to accomplish it, and more about the willingness to enter into a season of unpredictability. Even if only for half of a year, the dividends of the experience have the power to reach into a lifetime. Most come away from the journey with a renewed vision of what is most significant. If one can roam in the mountains with only the most basic of provision, and yet feel so complete, what exactly is life being lived for off of the trail? Many find that they have been living to support a lifestyle that takes more than it gives. The extent to which the walk required few material goods and outside distractions seemed directly proportionate to the replenished wells of the inner life.

To hike for months on end is to become aware that it takes very little, in fact, far less than we ever could have imagined to be supremely satisfied. Taking pleasure in the perfect height and slope of a flat rock to sit after many tired miles with no even surface to rest; soaking swollen and overworked feet in a cold sunlit stream. The weight and wet of a two-liter Nalgene bottle just refilled with spring water, jewel-like in the sun. Tap water when it is sixteen miles from the last source and some person you'll never meet leaves refilled jugs at the next trailhead.

Somewhere in the midst of the trail I stopped to take in a view from a rock outcropping, the vista framed by trees that seemed to be breathing in the wind, murmuring the secret of their patience to stand and grow in one place, stretching deep roots like sinews into the ground that sustained its life. I stood and reflected that everything I needed to live was on my back. The view was mine, the firm rock beneath my feet and the vibrant sky overhead; I felt like the richest person in the world. The feeling seemed an invitation to yell as loudly as possible for all the inexpressible delights: the exquisite lonesomeness of the trail, the taste of pure air, the countlessness of green growing things; all to be enjoyed, and yet, all to be freely released, with no sense of loss—an experience of pure abundance.

Wealth is not having many possessions; wealth is contentment and the freedom to enjoy one's life as it is, even in process. We often define poverty by what we don't have, rather than riches by what we don't need to be supremely happy. For the hiker who revels in the raw beauty of the mountains, there is no shortage of wonder, and that in itself is great treasure. *A man's life does not consist in the abundance of his possessions.*[24]

---

[24] Luke 12:15

Faith is not the clinging
to a shrine but an endless
pilgrimage of the heart.

Abraham Joshua Heschel

ten | Perseverance

There is great joy in taking one's physical being to its natural limit through the course of the thru-hike. It is hard to explain what makes the trail a longed-for experience after the fact in spite of the pains involved in backpacking, but it is akin to a yearning for home. Backpacking is really not about carrying a pack at all—yet it is the means of transport for something richer and deeper than just physical mobility and independence. Usual standards of comfort and convenience suspended for the most basic of needs have a way of making entrance for the spiritual.

Walking in the green tunnel of the tree-canopied trail hour after hour naturally can induce a meditative state. However, when weather, sore body and trail conditions all seem to point to being anywhere but the trail, resolution is needed to keep the sails full of air and going the right direction. Keeping eyes on the prize makes endurance possible. It is in the times of questioning that sometimes the best a hiker can do is to remember what put feet on the trail to begin with.

The essential attitude going into an endeavor is that whatever it takes, it will be done. Efforts sown in deprivation are harvested in abundance. Remembering what brought one to the trail in the first place is what allows the hiker who chooses to stay on the path to finish the course. A thru-hiker learns to thrive on a degree of mystery; to not be afraid of the unknown quantity of another day spent in the middle of the woods in the middle of nowhere; who knows or is at least learning the delicate balance between relying on self and others to keep to the trail.

At night before falling asleep gazing through the mesh ceiling of my little tent up at the stars, or lying on a shelter platform with other lavishly grubby characters, I would sometimes imagine the entire trail as seen from far above:

all the people heading north, south, out for a day, a week, a month, or half a year: but all moving along, expecting to find something of worth in the woods. Much legwork and many calluses, bruises and blisters later, one arrives at a place of completion. The end is usually if not always a predetermined state of mind.

Process

To find oneself further down the trail each day is a small miracle easily overlooked; self-propelling is a simple but profound pleasure. We often don't realize the progress we are making because change can happen in such small increments. However, while completion is what ultimately gets recognized, every point along the way is of the completed essence, and is to be celebrated. At times, seeing each small step as irreplaceably valuable is necessary just to keep it going.

The trail holds no judgment and is at once the foundation and atmosphere for all of the unquantifiable efforts made along its winding way. The impartial sun pours glorious angles over the mosaic of leaves and lives all caught up together in the same day's push forward. One person's process is not like that of any other, nor should it be judged. What matters along a parallel journey is that we increase our capacity for understanding others. That which cultivates renewed vision along the way is essential to any true progress.

It is one thing to be inspired by somebody and quite another to judge our path by another, which can lead to self-doubt or even self-rejection. Friendly competition promotes enthusiasm for one's own journey and allows us to celebrate that of another; we all stand to inspire and be inspired. But a sense of inadequacy regarding our own process or abilities can come when we only look through the lens of our aspirations, and neglect what is unique about our own walk. Like a puzzle piece with a specific shape that completes the whole, there is no greater joy than embracing who we are and doing what we were uniquely created to do—even though we are all still figuring out exactly what that is as we go.

How one walks the trail? Carefully, sometimes. Thoughtfully, usually. Occasionally, carelessly. Regardless, there is a daily internal dialogue with the physical path that mirrors one's inner life and workings. On the days the burden of thought seems far heavier than the backpack, scarred rock and stubborn roots in the way seem to offer up still greater resistance to moving on. Stumbling up a grueling, viewless ridgeline is often accompanied by such a bevy of head noise, it can be surprising trailside trees and plants are not bending away from the warpath of blue thoughts.

Nevertheless, purposing to complete the trail drives everything: walking with blisters, getting muddy in the rain, being an insect snack bar, braving the noxiousness of one's socks. Yet it is these less-desirable elements, or perhaps the resistance to such, that goads the psyche to experience the beauty that is beyond the momentary discomfort to the beauty of uncomplicated passage through the woods.

When the way seemed mercilessly steep yet again after many miles of climbing, I would sometimes yell to whomever and whatever might be listening: "the Appalachian Trail has officially become 'The Appalachian Trial'!" There was something oddly empowering about making it a public pronouncement, even just to the forest. No amount of wanting something different at the moment would change the weather, the treacherously steep, muddy slope, the meager supply of water till the next source, the separation from close trail companions up ahead or fallen behind. The only choice was to keep walking, despite the painful Achilles tendon, an aching knee, cold rain. Far less bearable than enduring the moment is abandoning it for the comparative tastelessness of not trying. Another oft-repeated phrase in response to the unfounded tendency to want to curse the mountain or the elements causing such a test was: "The trail owes me nothing."

While there is a complete and utter lack of certain options and conveniences on the trail, this kind of simplicity keeps things uncluttered. Excessive choice is not always advantageous. Most discover that it is enough to have strength and food and clothing and a reason to be there, to be fully participating. The days are full, and nothing seems lacking when there is just enough of what is needed; there is not room for more. It takes some time to develop this perspective, but at the end of the day, it is what works.

Exposure to anything for long enough can suddenly bring unexpected breakthrough. Water wearing down a rock over time can alter the shape of what would otherwise seem to be intrinsic and immutable properties. A negative attitude can lift with a conscious decision to shift one's mindset. The intricacies of the process nonetheless remain a mystery.

The Journey and the Goal

The trail is a powerful context for seeing the world beyond humanly engineered facades, inviting a look beyond the surface of things, past the fleeting acquaintance to a deeper draught of life. A plunge into the deep end.

Anticipation of trail's end accompanied every step like a companion; hope and action pointed like an arrow in the same direction, guided by the same purpose: completion of the goal. Though physically arduous at times, the walk was not difficult; in fact, seven months of walking the trail was the simplest existence I had ever imagined or experienced.

To not know what lies beyond the next bend reawakens a primal awareness that anything can happen at any time. Even the "rooms" of the forest constantly change; in one short mile the trees and forest understory can change into a different zone, from stands of ferns and birches to beeches to mature maples and tulip trees—an immense living kaleidoscope. Despite walking in what many refer to as the green tunnel, a certain predictability remains. Every day, mile upon mile of ushering oneself along the path adorned with countless life forms; the narrow little foot road freely strewn with unaccountable thoughts along the way.

The challenge of the trail lies less in complications of gear and itineraries and logistics, and more in embracing the freedom of those daring to move in unchartered regions, to move unencumbered by more common and unquestioned burdens.

No way or need to determine the end or the beginning of this kind of freedom; it was a cure for the common life, and passage to reawakening.

A View from the Trail

In the cool of the day, when dark shadows cast long and low over the mountains, stillness rises like cold, shaping a perfect composition of mud and silence, ice and lichen-clad rock. Water tumbles against rock rises, a vein of movement, a reminder that even what does not appear to move is still bound to an ancient rhythm, seen and felt in wind and water, cloud and the shifting reflection of a starry night through the changing seasons and the passing of each day. Mountains open wide their faces, sitting on wide haunches, yawning stone and wood back at the fiery sky overhead. Birds wing over crags, and trees bending over streams draw life-giving water to thirsting roots, their leaves whispering in the breeze.

More than witnessing the beauty of wildflowers and birdsong and patterns of light, fire and frost falling against branches in the sky held up by years of patient growth, the splendor of the trail is that perhaps for the first time, we are free of every other quest which seeks to define our existence. The narrowness of the trail ultimately liberates those walking it to let the hike be enough; no other agenda, nothing to prove, the past nothing more than a steppingstone to a life lived forward.

Katahdin

The days before trail's end were an exhilarating blend of anticipation and relief. Our weary, worn frames would soon be out of the cold, the path finally accomplished. Celebration was imminent, and for the past number of days, we spent hours fantasizing aloud as we hiked about the joys of car camping, Thanksgiving dinner, and indoor heat. Yet, despite all there was to look forward to, there was a growing sadness that the experience of a lifetime was about to come to an abrupt halt. The trail had turned our lives upside down, or more likely, right side up, but was this new beginning sustainable? Would things really be different after climbing one more mountain?

The joy of knowing that the goal of all the planning, the toil and all the miles was not only within reasonable walking distance, but soon within view, was dampened only slightly in those late October days by a streak of rainy weather. Guidebooks highlighted distinct spots where the majestic Mount Katahdin could be seen for the first time. One of the forthcoming views referenced was a dramatically picturesque setting by a lake. Eager to finally see what we had been walking towards all those long months, we reached the highly anticipated vantage point to see a complete washout of clouds that so utterly concealed the mountain it seemed to have disappeared into the lake.

We pitched our tents that night on a nearby peninsula in an insistent wind. The stars seemed to hang lower that evening, an audience of lights over our small cluster of trembling nylon shelters as we lay in silence listening to the cry of a loon, the haunting sound of perfect longing yet to be fulfilled.

Hours and miles later, we at last stood within view of the mountain—or at least, part of it. Thick clouds shrouded the topmost peaks, revealing only a narrow view of the very base of the mountain. Nevertheless, joyful resolve was near. Or so we believed. The intensity of our anticipation was about to clash with harsh reality a mere 5.2 miles from the end.

While Baxter State Park, the guardian of the northern trail terminus officially closes for overnight use in mid-October, exceptions were made for thru-hikers to stay one night and attempt a summit, weather permitting. Although a thin blanket of snow covered the ground, we were still confident of the final climb. What we didn't yet know was that while it was still largely autumn in the foothills, it was already winter in the higher elevations. Deep snow and ice pack were already forming, and all trails above tree line had been closed for several days. The mountain typically reopened the last month of the year after the ice was substantial enough for technical climbing.

Late in the afternoon, we finally stepped into the park, exuberant and giddy at a finish so close we could almost embrace it. We intended to spend one last night at a shelter within the park and climb to trail's end early the following morning; plans had been set in motion for family and friends to meet us at the end. Not even the slightest shadow of doubt existed that we were at the point of release; we were poised for celebration.

As we approached the shelter area, hiker friends we had not seen in weeks sat under the shade of the roof keeping warm in fleece and sleeping bags, their sober faces preparing us that the news was not promising. Apparently, we were further from the end than we had thought. Park rangers making the rounds had affirmed that no more summit attempts were anticipated until late spring the following year. They had just informed the waiting group that an ill-prepared citizen had somehow wandered into the park under their watch, and illegally climbed one of the mountain's steepest trails only used for technical climbing in the winter. He was fortuitously discovered by a mountaineer who found him in the final throes of hypothermia, just hours from death. The mood at the ranger station was understandably somber.

To have faithfully traversed the entire trail from Georgia to Maine to be told that the last five miles of over two thousand were not accessible due to just two days of poor weather was almost unbearable. But there were worse fates.

Not forty-eight hours before we had arrived, a couple of fellow thru-hikers managed to summit on a beautiful fall day, with no hint of the cold front on its way. Although the weather had taken a somewhat wintry turn, we were still optimistic of our own chances after our friends' recent successful climb. The dozen of us still clinging to the hope of summiting decided to take a few days in hopes of a shift in the weather. Taking respite from dire warnings that winter was in Maine to stay, we took refuge at a nearby lodge, reveling in the creature comforts of the great indoors. We still felt within range of just one more climb; after all, it was a short one at that. Perhaps our lengthy efforts and soon our patience would be rewarded.

With some deliberation, we chose day a week out for one first and final attempt up the mountain. If it didn't happen, we couldn't say we hadn't tried. There was always the spring. I kept my radical notions of taking a crash course in technical climbing to myself. After a full week of wintry weather, hopes had begun to ice over despite stalwart resolve to finish what had been started so many miles before. Nevertheless, we began strategizing our summit.

We were advised by a thru-hiking veteran from the previous year that we might have a better chance of getting to the top taking an alternate blue-blazed route which ultimately connected to the Appalachian Trail at Thoreau Spring, one mile from Baxter Peak and the terminus of the trail. The trail proposed was shorter and steeper, leading straight up through a boulder slide.[25] Some members of the group preferred to take the Appalachian Trail proper, though even purists often took such side trails as a concession in extreme weather. Discussions resulted in a decision to split into two groups. Half would pursue the white blazes, and the other half, the blue. I decided to follow the white blazes.

A Quarter Mile Away

Although the sky was bright and clear overhead, the trail nearing the summit was all but obscured by what was now several days' accumulation of snow. As we made our ascent, we paused for many photographs, tossed snowballs and took our time to savor what likely were the last few steps of an extraordinary journey. Finally reaching a boulder scramble a little more than a mile from the top, we attempted to hoist ourselves and each other up with the aid of rebar bolted into rocks now rendered treacherous by snow and ice, marking the farthest point we could reach. Taking several final photographs, we allowed the mountain to call it a day well done.

Convening at the lodge later that evening to share our summit attempts, we found that a couple from the group climbing the blue-blazed trail had come within a quarter mile of the summit, just close enough to catch a fleeting glimpse of the sign marking the trail terminus before clouds rolled in, obscuring the view. Both of these particular hikers lived in Maine. They had climbed the mountain many times, knew its many faces; the mountain was an old if not unpredictable friend. Yet wintry conditions made for a different kind of passage altogether. Cairns with blazes marking the trail were now hidden under nearly two feet of rime ice, looking like white wind-whipped waves frozen in place, their footsteps framed only by memory of the path.

Their decision to turn back when the clouds descended had been nothing but prudence. Had there been even limited visibility to the summit, losing it on the way back was a treacherous risk. A little more than a mile from the summit spreads an immense tableland, a topographical anomaly from the

---

[25] This turned out to be the same trail where the compromised hiker was found hours from death by the mountaineer.

perspective of the hiker who has undergone a nearly vertical climb to reach it. From lower elevations, it appeared like a kind of immense stoop for clouds to gather, a potentially deadly environment for a climber on a trail that had been silently, seamlessly erased.

Two Journeys Come to a Close

After sharing our respective stories of summit attempts, I called home to see how my grandfather was faring, now in the care of hospice. When he heard from his caregiver that a sizable group of us had been waiting out the weather to finish the trail, and that the rangers had told us that we might as well go home and come back in the spring to finish, his response had been: "You tell her I'd climb that mountain if it meant losing my fingernails and toenails to do it!" So very appropriate coming from the first human who had taught me as a small child that some people are to be respected with a healthy fear. And now, here we were, standing so close to completion at the terminus of two very different trails, yet so clearly aligned in spirit. What sweet fellowship, knowing we waited hand in hand despite the grief and joy, miles and years that separated us.

The terminus was near, but the end still unknown. The desire for a triumphant stand by that legendary marker had long seemed the trophy of the trail; to leave without this longed-for ceremony still seemed unthinkable. However, we had no choice but to adjust our expectations to live with the reality that we had indeed faithfully walked over twenty-one hundred miles from Georgia to Maine, Mt. Katahdin notwithstanding—and that might need to be enough.

Even as a prayer for wisdom was offered up, our meager chance of summiting forced us to look into the true essence of the trail experience. Commitment to the course is what matters, is the true substance of the hike. No lack of a posed picture next to a sign declaring the fact of the hike was going to make it any less meaningful or any less walked. While I believed this in theory, I could not convince myself to abandon the mountain without the desired closure—especially after my grandfather's words. The others seemed content to call it done. Feeling no release from the experience, I was compelled to try again until convinced there was no chance of summiting—that is, and still live to tell about it.

Life Loom

Probably the most poignant memories on the trail, as with any experience, are those in which the loom of life seems ready to release the fibers so painstakingly guided into place, and all that has been invested is about to unravel. It is then the brilliance of color and the intricacy of the pattern is most acutely seen, and we come back from a restored work with handfuls of insights won from the brink of loss. These are the spoils of war; but regardless of outcome, the real reward is the ability to *count it all joy* whether or not we stand at the coveted peak.

It was frustrating beyond words that instead of celebration, all the work and all the agony had come to grappling with the choice not to be bitter about being denied the chance to summit. And yet, my overriding desire was to not leave the mountain harboring anything but gratitude for the immense gift of the trail. To have had the time, resources, and the necessary limbs to walk was reward all its own. Channeling every effort into one singular focus and the events which are called into being by one's presence there was an honor. To simply be available to all that the walk can possibly offer is a tremendous gift, and it is more than enough.

Necessary Footprints

Early the next morning, three of us rode our zeal back into the park and against better judgment to make another summit attempt. Clouds were thick, visibility was going to be low. The going was extremely slow, and despite the considerable effort required to hike up such a severely vertical incline, low temperatures intensified by a bracing wind made for a demoralizingly cold effort. We made it over the top pitch, the vast tableland stretching before us like a moonscape. One of the hikers who had made it farthest the previous day led our tiny expedition, and with his lead we took turns surrendering our walking sticks, driving them one by one into the snow until the last was barely visible at intervals to mark our way back. The gravity of the situation settled in as we moved on in fog and silence.

Footprints left by the others from the day before were still evident and all we had to find our way across the frozen expanse. Our supply of walking sticks lasted just to the sign marking Thoreau Spring, one full mile from Baxter Peak; one mile from trail's end.

We snapped some photographs by the sign, poking the thick shell of rime ice off into the snow to read the letters etched deeply into the weathered wooden marker. Looking closely I was suddenly aware it really wasn't intended to be read under such conditions; it was as if we had cracked some sort of secret code. But it was clear we were leaving again without a visit to the very top.

The decision to leave in peace had been sealed the night before, and released as I climbed. I no longer expected anything from the mountain, and I left with the others with a sense of resignation and strength, satisfied that we could choose to walk away and be no less complete with the experience than had we accomplished a traditional summit on the brightest of days.

The Edge of Light

It was a lesson I had been presented with time and time again. An anonymous register entry at the shelter marking the halfway point on the trail had expressed it well: "Faith is walking to the edge of all the light you have and taking one more step." The irony was that to fully enter into the experience required its complete surrender.

I called my parents awaiting word of the summit attempt from Boston. Upon hearing all was done, they drove up to meet us at the lodge that very evening. Over dinner, I regaled them with all the hair-raising stories I'd vowed not to disclose before finishing. At the very least, and perhaps at its very best, the experience had peacefully concluded. Or so I thought.

Waking at dawn the next day, I pulled the shade, and in leapt the brilliance of a cloudless morning: the first after eight foggy days. I stepped across the quiet hall and nudged the door to my parents' room open a crack. "We're climbing." I have no memory of saying the words; all I know is that I expressed my desire and intention to try one more time. Judging by my mother's clear rememberance of what I actually said leads me to believe my spirit knew something my mind didn't.

I knocked on every remaining door in the lodge to find if anyone else wanted to try again, but only one hiker, Yukon Cornelius,[26] expressed interest in joining me in what the others regarded as a setup for one more disappointment. About half of the group had already left for home. I was convinced we were standing on the brink of the boundless treasure of one more chance, the cost only what might be encountered along the way in the attempt. A sense of guilt washed over me, now afraid that I would be the only one to enjoy what we all had walked so far and worked so hard to claim.

---

[26] Yukon's trail name was for the mountaineer in 'Rudolph the Red Nosed Reindeer' who helps a character lost in a blizzard find their way. A very appropriate moniker for this extraordinary hiker and friend; I could not have made my way through the snow and ice pack to the summit alone.

This is Your Hike!

I expressed this to one of the trail veterans awaiting her flight out the next day. She was resolute about only walking past the official white blazes, and therefore was not even slightly interested in taking an alternate route to the summit, which was hardly a given anyway. Small of stature but enormous of spirit, she was not one to be trifled with. When I mentioned that I was even considering not making the attempt out of respect for the other hikers, her eyes snapped as she said in characteristically impassioned tones: "Mogo! Do you know why you've been here eight days waiting for weather to clear before you could really hike that mountain? You still needed to learn this lesson! You came out here to hike this trail, and no one is going to do it for you! You get out there and hike! This is *your* hike!"

Here was the challenge: was I going to listen and follow what I felt called in my heart of hearts to do? Looking back, I was slightly horrified at how close I had come to trading my deepest longing for the dregs at the bottom of a cup which was not mine; to forfeit my hike for those who had chosen differently.

Regardless of what my actions provoked in another, it was not for me to try to change them. To simply let others react as they choose is giving them the freedom to do so. But it is a gift I must first give to myself. The trail was a tenacious teacher, down to the final moments. Looking out the window one last time, I made my decision. For the first time, the entire mountain could be seen. Clouds which hung like a curtain halfway down the mountain during our entire wait had finally lifted.

With my father driving the getaway car, always up for an adventure, Yukon and I made the hastiest dash to the park to make the most of the day. Leaving the pavement for the rough network of dirt roads throughout the park, we were finally at the trail head. A ranger who happened by as we prepared for the climb informed us to use caution as a storm front was swiftly moving in. He didn't ask how far we intended to go, but it was clear from his instruction as well as his demeanor that he knew exactly what we were attempting. It seemed one more opportunity to surrender the outcome of our attempt. But if we were meant to take the peak, how could it be prevented?

After a quiet entrance into the trees, the ascent began. The sky overhead increased in intensity to a bright, deep indigo until it appeared almost purple in hue.[27] The snowy path offered its brilliance sunward at intervals as we tattooed an irregular path with our tired boots and walking sticks.

I carried the thought of my grandfather on his own "trail" as we moved up higher and higher into the blue. Evergreens fat with snow and berry bushes with bright fruit perfectly outlined under icy caps of white bordered the trail. The way led straight up, a snowy ladder to a sacred height. The air was as quiet as it had been bracing the previous day. Soon I was tying my jacket around my waist in the still, sun-drenched air.

We clambered towards the finish we could almost taste, moving as if in a dream. Snow all but concealed the numerous boulders of the slide, making for curious lumps with pockets sometimes several feet deep, set like traps; knee-deep, then suddenly waist-deep. We were far too elated to care much; still, the way was frighteningly steep. Time was of the essence; the cloud front could be seen moving in from the west, and there was much ground to be covered. The advancing cloud bank was like an hourglass with the sand swiftly pouring.

When it seemed the trail couldn't get any steeper without curling back on itself, we reached the tableland. The clouds were now alarmingly close, but the sky directly overhead was clear and bright. We made it easily to Thoreau Spring, following the previous days' footprints, pausing to catch our breath and soak in the delicious moment of knowing that today, the gates of the mountain stood open. Onward!

No sooner had we begun our teetering progress over the rime ice[28] that grabbed our heels and held ankles and shins with every effort-filled step, the only visible trail made by the puncture of hiker tread suddenly stopped. The dazzling, unbroken spread of land lay before us, with no trace of a path, no footprints to follow. The sinking sense that there was nowhere to go, and no time to get lost or to find our way out began to settle in as we scanned the horizon, searching for any clue, any direction to the summit.

In the distance, several dramatic peaks seemed to present themselves as the direction to head toward. I hungrily, hopefully recalled the words of the

---

[27]   Showing photographs of the climb sometime later to a veteran New England hiker, not knowing when the photos had been taken, his comment was: "that looks like November sky [in Maine]." The date was November 8th, 1998.

[28]

hikers two days before who had made it just beyond Thoreau Spring, just close enough to see the sign. As I looked more closely, I spotted several large and consistently spaced lumps of snow on the closest of the peaks: cairns![29] If we could make it that far, surely we could see to the end. We began to run pell-mell through the snow, slowing to an exaggerated goose step to clear the mounds of rime ice committed to keeping our steps sluggish and methodical, like trying to run in a dream when the atmosphere seems to have taken on the viscosity of gelatin.

As we approached the snow-covered cairns, my eye was drawn to one in particular that seemed rather—square? Surely, the trail extended to the farther, more prominent peak; the sign couldn't possibly be that close; our vantage point was so limited, and there was no guidebook for navigating this kind of terrain. There was nothing to lose but time in heading in the general direction of the curious-looking cairns that resembled low-hung clouds frozen in time to the spine of the mountain. We scrambled on with renewed vigor, still heading for the farther peak, convinced that by the time we reached the last visible cairn, we would see others markers extending all the way to the sign. But we were in for another surprise.

A few steps more, and it was clear: we were heading straight for what could only be the terminus marker. Rime ice had so entirely overtaken the sign, no part of its humble, scarred structure underneath was even visible. An incredulous sense of fulfillment, relief, and ecstatic peace welled within as we stood not only in view but now directly in front of what seemed to be an almost otherworldly sight.

Never had a sight filled me with such unutterable joy—wonder—gratitude: the journey complete, all the more magnificent for what had been a long awaited and increasingly elusive end. The physical view seemed a perfect reflection of the inexpressible moment, awash in sparkling snow, golden blue sky and sun.

After taking a few pictures, a look to the western sky made it clear we had little time to spare to make it safely off the mountain. With what felt like a lifetime of pressure lifted, Yukon and I euphorically made our way across the tableland, and back over the steep Abol pitch, laughing and sliding on our backsides most of the way down the mountain.

---

[29] Cairns are rock piles placed at strategic intervals typically used to mark a trail above tree line.

Emerging from the woods and stepping back into the parking lot where my father had painstakingly awaited our return, he later said there was no need to ask if we had reached the top: our faces told the story.

After the ride back to Boston, it was hard to believe that the journey had finally drawn to a close. No words can describe the gift of having the chance to speak with my grandfather one last time and tell him the trip had concluded the very way that we had both so longed for. His exact and only words: "Thank you! Thank you! Thank you!" He passed away peacefully in his sleep the following day. Two souls were at rest.

A Few Questions

Most hikers' experiences along the Appalachian Trail are extraordinarily simple; the greatest wonder is the chance to see beauty in what is most present and easily overlooked. The trail is a context for seeing the world beyond humanly engineered facades, inviting a look beyond the surface of things, beyond the fleeting to a deeper acquaintance with life. Walking with a full backpack through rugged terrain with variables of weather and stamina is an ingenious handicap for slowing the pace and actually seeing the world pass by.

What is the Appalachian Trail? The Appalachian National Scenic Trail, commonly referred to as the AT is a continuous footpath of approximately 2,179 miles, tracing the spine of Appalachia across fourteen states from Georgia to Maine. Though it was "only" 2,160 miles in 1998, various trail relocations and land easements cause its exact length to change a bit every year. A running joke is that the sign announcing the midway point should be on wheels since the exact mileage can change several times in the course of a year.

The trail was completed in 1937, the conception of conservationist Benton MacKaye. His initial vision was to create a walking path between rural resorts in the Appalachian Mountains offering city dwellers retreat from the soul-quenching industrialism of post war urban America. Marathon attempts to walk its entire length were not part of the original concept, but in 1948, without fanfare or publicity, the first person walked end to end. A native Pennsylvanian and veteran of the Second World War, Earl Shaffer needed time and space to process, to heal—and what better sanctuary than the mountains, heading towards a definitive if not challenging goal. His accomplishment was not initially recognized by the Appalachian Trail Conference, formed by MacKaye and committee to maintain and protect the trail corridor. When Earl presented photographs and journals chronicling the walk, disbelief turned to accolades for what had not been thought possible.

What exactly is a thru-hiker? 'Thru-hiking' is the term used for a continuous end-to-end hike of a trail; 'thru-hiker' is the term used to describe the slightly mad individual attempting, usually fueled in part by inordinate amounts of Snickers bars. Typically about ten percent of those who begin also finish. The long-distance hike is a continual collision of shifting variables: weather, diet, injuries, family emergencies, all intensified by traveling in remote areas with little evidence of the world beyond tree and ridgeline, even when it is quite close. Not everyone has the time, interest or inclination to hike end-to-end, but most who do are aware that it is nothing less than grace that makes it happen.

How did you decide to walk the trail? Thru-hiking was not much more than a gradually developing dream for several years, following my first backpacking trip. Plans for other longish backpacking trips had been thwarted for one reason or another, each time only increasing my desire to go, though my initial dream was just to survive a month in the wild, not half a year or more. Then, at some point, a friend and I began discussing the feasibility of taking a two-month leave from work to hike a section of the Appalachian Trail. Dreaming turned to scheming, and plans gradually evolved to taking a half-year to allow time for a thru-hike.

Did you walk alone? The picture of a marathon is somewhat helpful to describe the movement of the thru-hike; crowded at the beginning, gradually thinning out as hikers settle into pace or leave the trail. Several weeks into the hike, my hiking partner and I decided to divide the gear we had been sharing to save weight, bit by bit replacing until we were mutually self-sufficient. By that time, we had naturally fallen in step with similarly-paced hikers. As northbounders, it was next to impossible to hike truly alone as the majority of the hiking pack continues to migrate towards the goal. By the time I reached New Hampshire, I realized that while I spent countless hours hiking in the day alone, I had never actually camped alone. I wanted to test my bravery, and set out alone for two weeks. Although I occasionally had the company of other hikers during the day, by the end of the two weeks I was ready to hike in a group again. The company of other thru-hikers made all the difference in having the morale to finish when the weather took a turn near the end of the trail.

Did you use walking sticks? Most people hike with walking sticks; to use them is to relieve hundreds of pounds of pressure from the knees over the course of a long-distance hike. Some invest in high-tech aluminum or titanium trekking poles; others harvest them as they go. I chose my sticks along the way, enjoying the ongoing project of whittling them smooth in camp at night.

What did you do when it rained? From the beginning of the hike, the choice was made: you came to walk, and that's what you do—with little exception. It rains, you walk. The sun shines, you walk. Hail and lightning, you walk through it. That said, the decision about whether to stop in one town or wait till the next to resupply is easily made under a quickly darkening canopy of clouds. Deciding to push on to the next shelter or quit for the night is easier made on a wet afternoon. Walking fifteen miles in the mud and having a better attitude at the end of the day than when the first drops splashed down is triumph.

How many blisters did you get? Until I experienced it for myself, I didn't believe those who said blisters were highly preventable on the trail. The key is to have a well-broken-in pair of boots before beginning, which thankfully, I had taken the time to do. I developed exactly three blisters on the trail: two were completely avoidable, and one was debatable. Blisters are produced primarily by heat, not friction. Once the heat from the friction causes a blister to develop, continued friction doesn't help matters, but it is not the blister's cause. The moment a 'hotspot' is felt, if covered immediately, it typically never progresses. Moleskin became a close friend those early days on the trail; though some find duct tape works just as well.

What did you eat and how did you resupply? When not foraging for berries, this was a function of passing through a town. Typical pack-friendly foods include dehydrated dinner mixes, dried fruit, nuts, bagels, cheese, jerky, energy bars and Snickers. Along with typical fare, I usually packed an apple and a few plum tomatoes or mushrooms which withstood riding in the backpack for a few days. Supplying at stores along the way worked for the most part, although choices were limited in smaller towns. I was more interested in having my freedom than a great selection of food. Dependency on the hours of the local post office to pick up supplies required more schedule keeping than I cared for in the woods.

Foods that could not be sustained for obvious lack of refrigeration were especially sought after in town, and on a few rare occasions, on the trail.

Near the trail's halfway point, a small campground store runs a racket known as the Half Gallon Club (HGC). I had never thought of my penchant for sweets on the trail as a form of gluttony, but it is understandable some would not comprehend the need to take pride in scooping one's way to the bottom of an entire carton of ice cream at one sitting.

Hiking with other newly inducted HGC members not long afterwards, one of our group was several miles up ahead. Oasis and I came to the last road crossing before reaching the day's destination and had the same thought: we would attempt a quick hitch into town and surprise our compadre with ice cream, his favorite food. Hitches are not always easy to come by, particularly in tandem. Half-jokingly, Oasis stuck her thumb out just as a pick up was passing by. She was still in the midst of saying "Let's just wait one minute and if no one comes by, we'll move on," as the truck screeched to a halt. We climbed in and bounced down the road perched on top of some old tires to the town's little general store. Walking out of the store with our prize, and time being of the essence, we asked the first person we encountered for a ride back to the trailhead, and within minutes, we were back on the trail. Well-wrapped in a foam sleeping pad, the ice cream was successfully smuggled without our companion's notice or suspicion, to his perpetually ravenous hiker heart's delight, just before it melted.

Did you carry any weapons? Only if you consider a classic Swiss army knife with toothpick and tweezers a weapon. The one tiny blade was particularly handy for slicing apples and cheese. The tiny scissors were perfect for cutting Moleskin patches.

Did you see many wild animals? When sleeping in the shelters, it was not uncommon to hear mice scampering, and occasionally be a runway of sorts for their acrobatics. Amazing how such a tiny creature can be so enormously destructive. It was necessary in the shelters to 'mouse-proof' one's food bag by hanging it from the rafters; even so, it was not uncommon for the more industrious ones to chew their way through not only food bags, but corners of sleeping bags, rain gear or backpacks, leaving a notorious signature in the form of an expertly shredded thatch of material behind.

I saw six bears on the trail—though not all at once.

The first spotting was of a bear loping through the woods at a lower elevation than the trail; close enough to watch, but far enough away to feel safe. The second bear sighting was three at once, and a myth buster, or at the very least an anomaly. Two of us were rounding a bend in the trail and there they were: a mother bear and her two cubs. Apparently as surprised as we were, the cubs turned about face and clambered up a small tree as the mother turned paw and scrambled away in the opposite direction! We tactfully backed away around the previous bend in the trail and waited a few minutes, scratching our heads about what we'd just witnessed.

The next encounter was rather unnerving. I was hiking alone and approaching the north entrance of Shenandoah Park when a dark shape to the left caught my notice. I looked to see a large bruin sitting on his haunches watching me closely not fifteen yards away. As I continued walking, he straightened to full height: impressively and intimidatingly large. Remembering advice to keep a visual barrier of trees between a bear and oneself to obscure the line of sight, I moved as quickly and quietly as I could manage with my heart thumping and ears dialed in for any tell-tale sign of the big bear making his way toward me; only the slightest rustling of wind in the leaves was heard.

The final sighting was a little disarming. Setting up camp along a rocky ridge in New Jersey late one night just as the high bush blueberries were ripening, I pitched my tent in a tiny cove surrounded by what seemed to be mountain laurels. The encircling branches seemed to add a degree of protection to the campsite, even if only visually. When I awoke at dawn and crawled out of my tent, there on a rock outcropping not ten yards away was a mid-sized bear pulling the blueberry bushes to his face, clearly too absorbed in his feast to pay attention to the incredulous human. I suddenly noticed that the "mountain laurels" around my tent were actually heavily laden with blueberries.

My first poisonous snake sighting was within the first week of the hike. It was dusk, and I was just steps from the shelter. A slight movement in the foliage inches from my feet caught my attention. Using my walking stick, I carefully parted the leaves, expecting to see some cute, furry or feathered creature, but to my surprise, it was a neatly coiled copperhead. I withdrew my walking stick and moved away as non-obtrusively as the snake itself was quietly hidden in the leaves.

Black snakes are commonly spotted along the trail, sometimes looped in the rafters of the shelter on mouse patrol, but as far as poisonous vipers, I probably saw more warnings than the snakes themselves. It was not uncommon to encounter a soggy piece of notebook paper with blurring ink in the middle of the trail held in place by a little rock with a hastily jotted warning about a viper sighting, for example, hanging out of a tree "five yards off the trail to the west;" not exactly comforting when the note had no date or time and no snake was in view.

How short did you cut your hair on the trail? Within a quarter inch of my scalp. When I began the hike it was too short to pull back into a pony tail, and as I didn't like wearing a hat to keep it out of my eyes, off it came. I figured six months of walking would be plenty of time to grow it back. It symbolized a season of measured risk, the dare of the journey with no holds barred and the end of a long, difficult season made ready for a new beginning.

How many miles did you hike in a day? My shortest day on the trail was about a dozen feet, the longest, 26 miles. My pace along the trail was neither fast nor slow. I hiked faster than some, slower than others. I never thought of myself as particularly speedy; there was too much to see and enjoy along the way. I was reminded that speed is relative when a hiking partner's friend came out for a visit when a particular pack of us had reached Vermont. We only hiked together for about a day, but I was amused by repeated remarks that I kept up a blistering pace. Perhaps there actually was something to show for that fact that I'd been hiking eight hours a day for five months with thirty pounds on my back.

The longest day was when Nocona, Two Showers and I decided to walk from Catawba to Troutville, Virginia: a marathon in the woods. Like many events on the trail, it was at least in part driven by the hiker's never-ending quest for more food. We'd had the misfortune to arrive the one day the highly acclaimed Home Place restaurant was closed. We compensated by devouring home style pizza stacked ridiculously high with every possible topping available in the deli of the small general store. After a luxurious night's rest in a dry and spacious U-Haul trailer parked behind the store, we lingered until late morning, chatting with other resupplying hikers coming and going.

Perhaps just three miles out of town, I could not stop thinking about cheese, and suggested we walk to the next town in order to plan the next food event. It was almost preposterous to suggest at such a late hour in the day, but the cause seemed worthy enough, and we were all in agreement. About halfway into the long day, we stopped for a supper break at the shelter that would have been the logical stop for the night. Hikers were settling in for the night as per usual. When the three of us began to shoulder our packs again for the second leg of the journey, one hiker piped up and asked us why we would want to go on a "death march." It was uncharacteristic to hear such gloomy words from the typically high-spirited thru-hiker community, but we were clear about our mission, and went on our way.

Not long after nightfall, rain began to fall and my headlamp proceeded to burn out. Picking my way in the darkness while relying on the gracious attempts of the other two to turn around and share their beam of light on the long, steep descent of crumbled, shifting shale that extended towards the end of the hike made for a slightly more challenging walk than desired. However, not having my own light that night turned out to have an unusual advantage. As I was spending even more time than usual scrutinizing each footfall, I caught sight of a bit of phosphorescence just off the footpath in the leaves on the ground that surely would have been missed under normal circumstances. I stooped for a closer look. I questioned my eyes as much as my sanity when I saw that it was, to my great astonishment, a glowworm! Until that precise moment, I'd assumed such creatures were fictional. My hiking partners laughed at my city-born lack of "sophistication" regarding such fauna.

Within a mile of our twenty-sixth on the final descent to town, the eerie sound of crackling power lines gradually increased in volume. As the path crisscrossed a tree line cut, we wondered if a line was down, and if so, would we even see it in the darkness? There was nothing to do but laugh at the increasing sense of absurdity as the hour drew well past midnight. When we finally stumbled into the motel office at the north end of our marathon, the innkeeper looked like he was seeing disembodied spirits walking in; about what we felt like.

How much weight did you lose? I gained twenty pounds. The average thru-hiker loses twenty-five. To clarify: the average *male* thru-hiker loses twenty five pounds. The typical female hiker's weight stays about the same, give or take a few pounds. The one exception is that women beginning the walk overweight tended to lose any excess; most others gained. The first time I weighed myself was at about the six week mark; it seemed I had been losing weight as I was becoming quite trim. But I was shocked upon stepping on the scale to find I had actually gained weight: twelve pounds, to be exact. "You women would last longer in a famine than we men, your metabolism is so much more efficient!" one hiker cheerfully remarked, not to my great delight.

Weeks later in southern Virginia, I hiked for a few hours with a previous year's thru-hiker who said she had packed only low-fat peanut butter on the trail to avoid unnecessary weight gain. While I completely dismissed it at the time, this turned out to be the strangest piece of counsel I wish I had heeded. At the time, I was not only eating whatever I wanted, but twice as much, and still getting in shape. It not only seemed ludicrous, but a sheer impossibility that anyone could actually gain weight while hauling anywhere from twenty to forty pounds up and down mountains all day long. By the time I reached Pennsylvania, I noticed I had put on some weight, and by the time I reached Maine, it was not only obvious to me. On my next similar endeavor, I will not be in denial about a woman's uniquely efficient metabolism. Bring on the peanut butter lite! Ah; maybe.

What was your least favorite part of the trail? Each section of the trail has its own charm or notoriety. A former zinc processing plant had all but wiped out a generation's worth of vegetation above Lehigh Valley in mid-Pennsylvania. We had spent the previous night in an impromptu shelter in the basement of the local police department known by the trail community as The Jailhouse Hostel. Bunks and showers and a ping-pong table were typical hostel fair, but its most unique feature was the way in the door: simply waving down a passing cruiser and asking to be let in the door. Among other things, it had the reputation of having the best shower on the trail, a perk second only to the best all-you-can-eat buffets, nicest hostels and most generous trail angels.

The next day, we walked out of town and back up into the mountains into what was the most unforgiving, harshest portion of the trail from start to finish. The path was fairly graded at first, and then came to a very steep climb up out of the town. It was a steep boulder scramble, and before long, we were in the midst of a scorched plateau. It was a blisteringly hot day in May, and there was no relief from the torrents of sunlight. Limbless trees long dead, bleached silver by many fruitless days in hot sun and wind stood like monuments to a distant past. As far as the eye could see in any direction, jumbles of tree limbs lay scattered over the terrain. The day we traversed this section was one of the most exposed stretches on the whole trail, brutal on a hot day, made more so by the utter lack of tree cover and lack of water sources. To top it off, we were weighed down with a full day's worth of water, which turned out to not be enough as it was. Rationing water in such conditions did nothing to endear the experience.

Despite the bleakness, there were signs of life: when least expecting anything growing in the midst of the deadness, colorful wildflowers could be seen peaking here and there between the wooden debris, a reminder of the relentlessness of life and hope after devastation.

What was the most difficult mile on the trail? What had a reputation of being the toughest also happened to be the most enjoyable. Described as a "jungle gym for giants," Mahoosic Notch is known as the most difficult mile on the entire trail. Car and small house-sized boulders are strewn along an otherwise relatively level area that requires taking one's pack off at times to squeeze through narrow passages on the way through. While a normal pace along the trail is around two miles an hour, the Notch, one mile in length, takes about two hours to traverse. I scrambled through the notch with two section hikers, experienced with bouldering and climbing, who coached the principle of three fixed points for stability. When the terrain is difficult, it often requires slowing one's pace to make it through. And at such times, maintaining stability and balance is essential: and to simply keep moving.

How many pairs of boots did you go through walking from Georgia to Maine? Three; one pair for each blister I incurred . . . treads wear thin, laces wear through, mud and dust have their way until the boots look like they've had ten years of use rather than ten weeks. It would be interesting to see the journey just from the boot-level perspective: swinging past countless plants and life forms, stepping each time onto a new patch of soil or ancient rock surface; splashing into another puddle after rainfall, and baking them dry again on the next sun-soaked hillside.

I learned that you sometimes get what you pay for—or that you can't be too prepared, or prepared at all for what is unknown. My boots were beginning to crumble away after the first eight hundred miles; as the sole had separated from the welt, it was almost impossible not to trip every few steps. I supposed I burned more calories walking that way. As the next town had a shoe repair shop, and I had grown to love my now slipper-comfortable boots (bearing scarred-over blisters from the difficult breaking-in process), I had high hopes they could be re-sewn. I will never forget the lecture the cobbler gave me after a quick survey of my expensive, Italian-made boots: "You young people don't know how to walk! You kick the rocks! Learn how to pick your feet up when you walk!" I wondered how far down the trail he'd ever walked, but I didn't bother to ask. After insisting there was nothing he could do for my boots, he nevertheless muttered that he would see what he could do. The repaired boots were expertly sewn, but were not long for the trail.

I purchased another pair on sale at a local outfitter; they seemed comfortable enough, and a good fit. What I didn't know then and couldn't have was that the right-footed boot was just a little too tight. The brand was one of the most popular on the trail, and I had no reason to doubt their trail-worthiness. They felt almost broken in upon first fit; not a small feat on the trail since there is no way around the blisters when there is no other change of shoes. The boots were lighter weight and more suited for mid-summer temperatures. A few days in, I was delighted to report no blisters. Yet, there was a growing sense of pressure on a tendon slightly below my left big toe. No pain, no indentation just some tension. It didn't seem anything serious, and since it didn't hurt, it was easy to ignore. Trying to loosen the laces did nothing to help.

About a week later, I met up with old friends in picturesque Harpers Ferry, West Virginia, known as the 'psychological halfway point' of the trail. The bruise on my foot where the boot was too tight had developed into a healthily-visible bump that another hiker, who happened to be a nurse, said needed to be checked out, although I was stubbornly prepared to keep walking on it. (On the trail, something is always hurting, and as one hiker remarked, as long as the pain shifts around, you should be okay to keep going.) Meanwhile, the small bump had grown to a cartoonishly prominent cyst. I had it taken care of at a clinic, and momentarily wore the old crumbling Italian boots after the swelling ruled out the now not so new pair of boots that had started the trouble to begin with. Graciously, the same hiking partner gave me a pair of boots that she had well broken in before the trail; what she could not have predicted is that swelling and fallen arches would result in needing one whole shoe size larger. The third pair of boots could not have fit better if custom made. By the time I reached Katahdin, they were more than ready to be retired, along with their owner.

Journal Randoms

When a chance encounter with an editor after the hike resulted in his encouragement to publish my trail journals, sure that the story was basically written already, I laughed, knowing seven months' worth of writing consisted largely of entries written over and over like: "Can't wait to get to town tomorrow and eat pizza," or "I'm so, so, so tired" or "I wonder if this rain is ever going to stop." Not particularly lofty insights, though typical of a thru-hiker. Had I intended to write a book before the hike, I would have paused throughout the day to write, rather than waiting until cocooned in my sleeping bag at day's end when attempts at meaningful reflection were competing with the need to rest.

But there is something to be said for the chance to have been fully immersed in the trail, with no agenda other than to move freely through the days, to learn again what it is to simply be. And even if nothing was eventually written down, nothing could ever take that away. As it is, what has been written hardly begins to tell the fullness of the experience.

~

We are lying here in the shelter four across, laughing at the most unbelievably silly things . . . so strange to actually be here . . . . amazing how all the talking and planning has borne this fruit. Thrillingly, I was warm and cozy all night, though minor aching and stiffness-nothing thwarting. A nice breakfast of cheese, bread and tea, a quick repacking, and we are ready to go. Beautiful rhododendron thickets during the first section of the day, passed some falls. Approaching the shelter here and seeing about fourteen hikers standing and sitting around was a little daunting at first, but it's apparent that most here are just starting out too, and therefore, pretty congenial. No intimidating "pros" to make me feel embarrassed at my lack of hiking/camping prowess. Hope to pick up some good habits with food prep. Ramen's going to get old pretty fast, I believe.

~

The only gap that you actually walk up to on the trail also marks the first state line crossing. The sense of celebration is palpable, and the catalyst is nothing more than a small three by nine-inch piece of wood nailed into a tree with the letters GA/NC somewhat crudely carved. But memorials are important, mile markers and signposts remind us of where we've been and where we are going. At camp tonight, we made a small fire, and all at once I looked up into the tree-tops to see a great horned-owl sitting above us, still as a sentinel. No sooner had I pointed it out to others, he spread his wings and fell away from the tree in silent flight, one with the night.

It's amazing how quickly a group of complete strangers can begin to feel like some weird kind of family of friends so quickly. My thoughts are peering towards the soft edge of sleep, and though it's only 7:35pm, think it's a darn good idea to give in to the urge . . .

~

The hike today wasn't too bad-rained steadily, slabbed around and around, steep drop-off on one side, steep incline on the other, clouds and trees woven together in damp grey light.

~

Is it possible to want for others, but not accept the same for myself? To want for others what I do not have?

~

The trail's path is traced by my footsteps, but the way threads itself through my entire being.

~

Last night was quite cold, but somehow managed to negotiate some slices of sleep between the chills. Chunks of ice hit my tent a few times, giving the impression of an impish prank on the part of somebody, but I guess that's just Georgia's way of fooling with sun and spring-hungry Northerners . . . felt right at home yesterday in the fog and icy sleet-so glad it isn't raining! It was so lovely twisting and turning through the white hallways of the forest, everything dazzling changed by frosty garb. Haven't unzipped my tent yet, but it almost looks like the sun's shining—one day closer to warm!

~

Before falling asleep, watched the fire spit sparks against the bright stars mingling with the night. I was truly cozy and warm, but the repertoire of snores didn't let up till dawn . . .

~

For whatever reason, I flew today; lots of ups and downs, but I had an energy that seemed to come from nowhere despite hurting, tired feet and sore back. (Funny how certain people aren't very familiar or enjoyable till others less familiar appear, and the formerly unfriendly unfamiliar seem friendly and familiar. Brilliant, eh?) Stream of consciousness has just kicked in. It's snowing and the fire at our feet is hot. Never written outside in the snow before, but I think I like it. Fire's a-glowing pinkish orange. In for another warm night, hopefully. I "need" a shower, bad. My boots are filthy dirty. I think I might be getting used to living outside. Gathered a bunch of firewood to keep warm in the two obvious ways. The snow is pretty steady now, so maybe I'll turn in. My not-so-eloquent thoughts have disintegrated even as my ink in this wet . . . Goodnight and amen.

~

Trying to ascend a particularly trying hill the other day, I suddenly perceived that God was telling me I'd been carrying a much heavier load than the one on my back for a long, long time: other people's loads.

~

Forgot to say yesterday: we've passed the first hundred miles? Seems like an accomplishment. Funny how out here, you just "do" things. This is my life now, this is how I live, and I am just doing it. Maybe as we go along and every aspect becomes more automatic, I will be able to reflect more on what this is. But till then, I am going to enjoy such a purely simple existence. The birds are singing and calling to one another high in the trees, and the air is fragrant with pine needles and newly growing things. (I'm afraid my clothing and my sleeping bag are fragrant with newly growing things, too-less pleasantly so . . .)

~

For those of you who miss Eden
Come walk through my valleys
Let your breath be the wind
in my hills, your laughter
mingling with the sweet air
Come sing with your eyes
your feet, your hands
over the shape of this land
Let yourself glide with the shadows
over the wrinkled mountains

~

Today on the peak of Rocky Top (yes, of balladry fame) reading a bit of "Sickness Unto Death," Kierkegaard describes the experience of feeling there is nowhere to progress, which leads to a kind of despair. Rather than only being negative, this despair can be extremely fruitful as it awakens us to our need for complete transparency and dependence upon God.

~

The way of the spirit is always an unexpected way.

~

I feel I could be happy being a reed or a grass bending in the wind—after all, what is there really to do? Most of what folks do seems to be held at bay or held together by something which is going to fall apart anyway.

~

The past is dead. It cannot move, it remains frozen in memory. It cannot of its own accord touch today. Yet we chisel pieces of the past and drop them, anvil-like, over tender today, and say, "Why is today so heavy and sharp?" It is not today which is so.

~

Pass through hallways of trees
towering stone
mosses, grasses' wet touch and
junco's small voice
dangling from a ceiling
of wind and leaves
Hungry eyes rove over this land

Silent and wholly content with
what the sky brings to sister earth
The caterpillar tread of the sun
marks the crush and groan of days
pressed foot by foot into the soil
Earth pushes up favor while
light pours down between
branches and blades of green
Even the downcast eye rejoices
to sweep such a path where
beauty blooms in humility
Some ask, what do you eat on the trail?
I eat the sun, I eat the fragrance of the great pine.
I eat the rain. I eat rocks big enough to dream on.
I eat roots stretched like veins over the hardy path.
I eat birdsong and windsong, I eat autumn leaves
and velvet moss—I eat with my skin, my nose;
I eat with my eyes the abundance of the woodland table.
Starlight hangs like loose, bright feathers
from black pinions of the sky
We lower our eyes into this dark ocean
of soundless music, caught in the space
between knowledge and wonder
"Be still and know . . ."
This vessel holds a thousand days in one day
A thousand beginnings, a thousand ends
Each marked by the fluttering of eyelids,
opening to life, closing in death
new emerging from the old
Birch tree pours off its bark
Pine tree spins, singing symmetry
Mouth of the spring quenches its own thirst

~

"Never forget that it is my strength that enables you
The very strength you've been given to a walk down the trail every day is from Me
You are vessels for my use—I will fill you
You cannot fill yourself, only I, and it is I who pours you out when it is time
You cannot pour yourself any more than a jar can pick itself up!
Just be open to Me, and I will fill you
I created you, just as I created the trees and the rocks
You have no idea how beautiful you are—remain open to be fully beautiful

I am truth—you will not be so bombarded by lies if you will look to me—I am the way, the Truth and the life—Truth
I who created the eye to see—I am sight, I am light! I am beyond sight, I am beyond light"

~

God will speak through whomever God chooses.

~

"Stubbornness is like a dead root in the ground. Let your roots grow strong and alive into a living vine. When dead branches are pruned, they are only cut in places where growth will occur more strongly."

~

Anger made me pitch my tent completely taut for the first time.

~

Revelation I am not sure what to do with—forgive me for loving and living for the ideal more than the reality.

~

Over-concern with what others think is a form of idolatry.

~

God has given us permission to make mistakes, though never without consequence, and good, too, has consequences.

~

Constant traffic on a foot path in the woods keeps the way clear—the moment something sprouts in the path, the next moment may find it stamped out. Likewise, continual prayer and digestion of the word will help keep our way clear.

~

The trail is a metaphor for life. The path is paved with the wind of an awakening heard deep within the soul.

~

Cool, crisp mountain air inhaled deeply; the dim crackle of fallen leaves mixed with snow tumbling together under boot tread. The pleasant feeling of a rhythmic gait as the trail passes quietly underfoot, allowing the mind a unique kind of respite.

~

There is no clinging on the trail—not to people—not to things. The walk is a practice in letting go.

~

One's pace is not hurried on the trail if sure footing is the goal. A twisted ankle can result even from well-intentioned placement. Many twists and turns make up the forward movement along the trail—and much patience required to calibrate body and mind and soul to this intricate, lowly pacing. So with the Spirit.

~

The earth wrinkles its way along under the watchful eye of moon and sun.

~

Birds and creeping things all tell their tales in myriad ways, never once stopping to ask why or to consider the plumbless depths of the wisdom on which the earth's foundation rests. The ancient voice thunders truth and meaning to transient yesterdays and uncertain tomorrows.

Epilogue

Capturing the essence of the trail in words proved far more strenuous than the hike itself; from start to finish it was a bushwhack of discovery through uncharted territory. But things have their fullness in time.

The end of the matter: expect the unexpected. Regard the days and hours given as sacred gifts, remembering that time does not return. The investment is here and now. If there is regret from opportunities lost, take heart knowing that other opportunities will come, and others can be created.

The trail is about entering in with complete abandon, in purity of will and desire, and the importance of walking alongside others who share the joy of becoming. It is about allowing the old to burn away in order to step into a vibrant new beginning—it is about awakening to the joy of a life lived to the full.

The way is narrow, it is focused, and best when simply followed. On to the next journey.

Above all, do not lose your desire to walk: every day I walk myself into a state of well-being and walk away from every illness. I have walked myself into my best thoughts, and I know of no thought so burdensome that one cannot walk away from it . . . but by sitting still, and the more one sits still, the closer one comes to feeling ill . . . Thus if one just keeps on walking, everything will be all right.

~Søren Kierkegaard

All photographs taken in 1998.

one | McAffee Knob, Catawba, Virginia
two | Smoky Mountain National Park, Tennessee
three | Woods Hole Hostel, Virginia
four | Purple, Shenandoah National Park, Virginia
five | Lonesome Lake, White Mountains, New Hampshire
six | Smoky Mountain National Park, Tennessee
seven | Bears Den, Bluemont, Virginia
eight | Mt. Washington, New Hampshire
nine | Spy Rock, Montebello, Virginia
ten | Mt. Katahdin, Maine

Edwards Brothers, Inc.
Thorofare, NJ USA
February 25, 2012